SECOND LIVES

Becoming a
Consultant

Also by Bill Harris

Second Lives: Becoming a Desktop Publisher
Second Lives: Becoming a Freelance Writer

SECOND LIVES

Becoming a
Consultant

BILL HARRIS

Introduction by Charles L. Sodikoff, Ph.D.

St. Martin's Griffin 🦅 New York

Library of Congress Cataloging-in-Publication Data

Harris, Bill
    Second lives: becoming a consultant / Bill Harris.—1st St.
Martin's Griffin ed.
        p.   cm.
    ISBN 0-312-20002-1
    1. Business consultants.   2. Consultants.   3. Career changes.
4. Self-employed.   5. New business enterprises—Management.
I. Title.
HD69.C6H373   1999
001'.068—dc21   99-15139
                                                           CIP

First St. Martin's Griffin Edition: August 1999

10   9   8   7   6   5   4   3   2   1

Contents

INTRODUCTION

Starting over? What does that mean to you? To some it means opportunity, challenge, and growth. To others it means danger and defeat. To everyone it means *change*.

Change is defining the course of America today. Millions of us who have spent the first part of our working lives employed by someone else are now—either unwillingly or by our own initiative—starting over. The options are clear: find another job in your current trade, find a job in a new trade, retire (if you can afford it), or work for yourself.

Second Lives is a guidebook for those who are considering using the experience and skills acquired working for someone else to go into business for themselves.

Going into business is like learning to ride a bike. Remember that first try? Someone held the bike and ran alongside. You pumped your legs as hard as you could, wobbling wildly as you tried to keep the front wheel straight. Then suddenly you were on your own, but you probably didn't get very far. Maybe you scraped your knees when you fell.

After that there were some more bumpy rides, falls, and scrapes, but eventually the ride smoothed out and a whole new world opened up. Our lives changed. We had more independence. We traveled to new places and did new things. We kept up with some of our friends and left others in the dust.

That's exactly what starting a new business is like.

Second Lives is the guiding hand on the back of your bicycle. It will help you make the decision as to whether or not to go off on your own; identify the type of business you ought to pursue; and give you the support to launch your business successfully.

Starting you own business may be the most exciting, but hair-raising adventure you ever take. I know, not only because I have counseled many people who have tried it, but also because I have done it myself. At age forty-eight, I decided to open my own consulting practice after years and years of working for someone else. The trip has been exhilarating and my second life has been the happiest of my entire career. Sure, there have been scary periods and times when I wasn't so certain I would succeed, but with a strong motivation, the proper skills, and the flexibility to adapt to the ever-changing needs of my business, I am well on my way.

I hope this book helps you make the right decision for yourself. If you do choose to go out on your own, put on your helmet and be prepared for the most exciting ride of your life.

—*Charles L. Sodikoff, Ph.D.*

SECOND LIVES

Becoming a
Consultant

CHAPTER ONE

A World of Your Own

At one time or another, just about everyone has had a dream of being self-employed. That may be your dream right now and if the job description that goes with it is "consultant," there has never been a better time to declare your independence. More and more companies of every size are trying to get by with fewer employees and most are finding that it can't be done without the help of outside consultants. The computer revolution has also created a need for consultants as companies are looking for help and advice to catch up and keep up with all of its possibilities.

But the opportunities for consultants aren't just limited to the business world. As everyone's life becomes more complex, people are willing to pay for help with just about everything from financial planning to putting a new wardrobe together to learning how to navigate the web, and the market for such things continues to grow.

The decision to go off on your own and take advantage of these new opportunities is going to take a great deal of soul searching. There's no denying that starting your own business takes a lot of courage. You'll be facing a host of stumbling blocks, one of the biggest of which may be the fear of change.

Most people find change frightening, but you might be surprised to discover that change really isn't unfamiliar territory.

Chances are you aren't doing your job in the same way as you did five or ten years ago and you've been dealing with change for a lot longer than you think. Back in your father's day, holding a job for twenty or thirty years often added up to one year's experience repeated twenty or thirty times. But experience is something quite different in today's world. You've probably seen it in your own career. Thanks to change, there are many facets to your experience, and that variety is going to make a big difference to you in your career as an independent consultant.

Another key consideration in your decision to begin your own business is the question of security. There are no guaranteed weekly paychecks or health benefits when you work for yourself. In fact, there are no guarantees at all. But keep in mind that, like change, security also has a new meaning today. Not too many years ago, people expected to retire from the same job they started out in whether they liked it or not. But companies have changed, and so have people. Attitudes have also undergone change. Nobody expects a job to last a lifetime anymore.

The silver lining in all this is that we're freer than we've ever been to try something new and change our lives. There may never have been a better time to put yourself in control of your own destiny.

YOU'RE NOT ALONE

Your independent consultancy practice is going to be your way of supporting yourself, and it will be up to you to produce enough income to make ends meet. When you are in the business of ideas, which is what consulting is all about, it's sometimes easy to forget that you, too, are running a business. It is important to keep in mind that when all is said and done, you are going to be in business for yourself just as surely as if you were opening a boutique or starting up a restaurant.

Many consultants eventually build teams, either by adding employees or by forging associations with other experts in their field, but most begin building their businesses alone with only themselves to rely on for everything from finding clients and solving their problems to following through to be sure their ideas are implemented. Even when you reach the point of adding associates to enhance your business, your practice will still be based on your experience and your personality. You will be the one in charge.

Being in charge of your own life is at the heart of the American Dream. It's the same promise that brought our ancestors here; it's what built the country, and it's what still drives millions of Americans. According to a 1997 survey by the Entrepreneurial Research Consortium, as many as 4 percent of American adults are in the process of starting up more than three million small businesses at any given time. The survey also revealed that one out of every three U.S. households—thirty-five million of them—includes someone who at one time or another has followed the dream of going into business for him or herself. It's happening all around you. Old people, young people, men and women, are walking away from unsatisfying nine-to-five jobs, time-wasting commutes, office politics, and unappreciative bosses.

Many of us have known them—bosses who were either unfair, unyielding, incompetent, insensitive, mean-spirited, double-dealing, or all of the above. That's no fun, and one of the reasons why you may have bought this book is because you don't want to spend the rest of your life working for people who sometimes seem to go out of their way to make life difficult.

Establishing your own business as a consultant will give you a chance to use the skills you've developed working for someone else to create a whole new life for yourself—only this time around it can be tailored specifically for you, with more freedom, interest, and satisfaction.

IT'S YOUR LIFE

Of course, it's pretty easy to talk yourself into staying put. You might be telling yourself that striking out on your own isn't a realistic thing to do. But consider one of the joyous realities of modern life: we're all probably going to live to see our seventy-fifth birthday, and most likely quite a few after that. Do you really want the second half of your life to be a carbon copy of the first? These days there so many different options and opportunities available for you to turn your experience and your skills into a marketable service, you'd be short-changing yourself if you don't explore what's out there.

Consider what's been happening in corporate America. Down-sizing leaves hundreds out of work; Wall Street cheers and the victims have anxiety attacks. The gurus of big business preach that getting rid of deadwood cuts a company's costs, the survivors work a bit harder, and stock prices go up. But there is only so much work a company can squeeze from its people, and its commitment to stay mean and lean usually means it can't hire new employees either.

That is wonderful news for consultants. In today's world, it's considered good business for companies to "go outside" and hire consultants both to get the work done and to help solve the problems they created for themselves when they cut back their payrolls. Whatever management thinks it can do without, there is no substitute for experience, and as a consultant that is your stock-in-trade.

FOLLOW YOUR DREAM

At some point in their lives, everybody has dreamed of making it big. Some do, and some just make their lives better. The first step toward making your dream come true is getting rid of the illusion that you need to play out the hand you've been dealt.

It's never too late to wipe the slate clean and take charge of your life. It's *your* life, after all, and there isn't any reason why it shouldn't be satisfying. If you think your own ideas are better, don't waste them on the suggestion box. Use them for yourself. You never know where they'll take you—until you try.

CHAPTER TWO

What Is a Consultant and How Do I Become One?

At one time or another, you may have met an old friend or associate and began the conversation by asking, "What are you doing these days?" If the answer was "consulting," you may have assumed it was a face-saving way of saying "I'm out of work," and changed the subject. But the fact is that it's a rare consultant who's out of work for long these days. Chances are good that if you had pursued the topic you'd have discovered that this person had found a better way of life and was very likely doing quite well, both in terms of job satisfaction and income—not to mention having the kind of freedom you are only dreaming about.

The word "consultant" practically defines itself, but describing a consulting practice is very much like blind men describing an elephant, and this elephant is one huge animal. About the only thing that all consultants have in common is that they offer expertise for hire. A freelance writer is a consultant, so is a desktop publisher, an interior decorator, or a computer programmer. A retired executive who helps younger CEOs solve management problems is obviously a consultant, but not so obvious is the contractor who comes up with ideas to help people remodel their kitchens. It all boils down to bringing experience to someone else's need.

Some professionals don't call themselves consultants at all, but not because they aren't. Lawyers and doctors, accountants and stockbrokers, for instance, don't usually think they have much in common with someone who makes a living as a professional management consultant; but in fact they do.

In the final analysis, they are all making their living from the things they've learned along the way. Sharing experience and using it to solve problems is at the heart of every consultant's practice. And the successful ones all have another thing in common—they never stop learning. Keeping up with change is what keeps their services in demand.

WHERE THE OPPORTUNITIES ARE

"At your service" is a slogan that fits every consultancy like a glove. It is a profession that satisfies just about any need that exists in the business and personal lives of potential clients. Your opportunities as a freelance consultant will be as endless as your experience, your accomplishments, and your own imagination. Among the fields that are producing successful consultancies, but by no means all of them, include:

Accounting	Construction coordinating
Advertising design	Customer service
Architecture	Data processing
Art and antiques	Desktop publishing
Banking	Direct mail
Business communication	Employee relocation
Child care	Employment counseling
Collection and credit	Environmental planning
Computer programming	Event planning
Computer training	Graphic design

Fashion consulting
Financial planning
Freelance writing
Fund-raising
Gardening
Home improvement planning
Insurance
Interior decoration
Landscape design
Legal research
Makeup consulting
Market research
Nutrition
Personal shopping
Personal training
Polling
Public relations
Public speaking
Résumé writing
Sales promotion
Sales training
Scholarship research
Security
Tax planning
Telecommunications
Transportation
Travel planning
Tutoring
Time management
Website design

When all is said and done, a consultant is simply someone whose experience is worth something to another who is looking for solutions to problems or a better use of his or her own time.

EVERY EXPERIENCE COUNTS

Michael Nelson, who has a successful consulting practice in Bloomington, Minnesota, worked his way through college with various restaurant jobs, and it turned out that he learned as much there as he did in the classroom. "I get bored easily," he says, "and I spent a lot of time exploring things like staff training that weren't part of the job." After he graduated, he tried a number of different jobs, from manufacturing plants to offices, moving from one to another and continually learning new things, but never quite beating what he perceived as the boredom of the jobs themselves. He says it made him a jack-of-all-trades, but the trade that he found most interesting was the restaurant business. While he was working for a company in the field, he began a sideline occupation as a restaurant consultant and worked at it part-time for three years before he turned it into a full-time business. When he worked at staffing for temporary agencies, Michael had become an expert on the intricacies of labor compliance and benefits programs and his experience made him valuable to companies in other fields as well. Today his business, which he calls The Solution Consortium, provides strategic planning and support as well as project management for clients as varied as lawyers and manufacturing company executives. Solving their problems was a heaven-sent opportunity to beat Michael's boredom problem. And his varied experience often adds up to exactly what a particular client needs. "Every company has a goal," Michael says, "but many of them don't know how to reach it. My job is to devise a plan that will make it possible." But he relies on more than experience to get the job done. "I never stop learning," he says, "and if I don't always know the answer, I do always know where to find it." The key to that is people, and Michael makes it a point to keep in touch as much as possible with people he's met along the way. As he puts it, "Every connection you make will come back." Networking is one of the best ways to find new business in any field, but in consulting it's also one of the best ways to find business solutions.

EVERY INTEREST COUNTS

Not every consultant is concerned about business solutions, though. Packy Boukis is much more concerned about such simple things as her clients' happiness. She is a wedding consultant in Cleveland, Ohio. Packy started her working life as a secretary, and when she became a mother, she switched to part-time jobs, including a sales job that required her to meet a weekly quota or get fired. She made it a point to be able to quit eventually, but not before she had polished a newfound skill of talking to people. It was another part-time job, working for a department store's bridal registry, that gave her the idea to go into business for herself. "I was looking for freedom," she says, "and after two years as a wedding consultant, I can say that I've found a lot more than that."

Helping brides and grooms ranks high among mothers of grown children as a possible business opportunity. Many have been mothers of the bride themselves, and once memories of wedding day pressures have faded, it seems as though getting paid for going to weddings might be fun. It can be, and it can be a profitable business too. But there is more to it than meets the eye. Patricia Bruneau, whose company, L'Affaire Du Temps, has been creating memorable days for Northern California brides for half a dozen years, points out that while the job is indeed fun, the word "fun" itself may be the most overrated one in the business.

"I believe that people who become wedding consultants because it looks like fun are the ones who are most likely to fail," she says. "It's a great business and I enjoy what I do very much. But it is also a full-time business. I spend approximately a hundred hours with each of my clients, and that doesn't include the time in the office, on the phone, or traveling. It is important to our profession that it is viewed as a business and not a 'hobby.' We are working with clients on the most important day of their lives and decisions have to be made in a professional and timely manner. It takes skill to deal with many different kinds of people and it takes good organizational skills as well. It also involves dealing with other professionals in the field, not just the bride and groom. And it involves running a gauntlet of emotions with the bride and groom and their families at different stages of the planning. Add it all up and then multiply it by seven or eight different weddings in one stage or another at one time and you'll understand why patience and efficiency are our most valuable tools."

On the other hand, there is no reason why having fun making

a living shouldn't be high on your list of reasons for becoming a consultant. It's one of the best reasons there is. Being a consultant, whether it's in the field of computers, traveling, or gardening, involves using skills and knowledge you're comfortable with, and when you do, your business becomes a pleasure. If you have a green thumb, for instance, think of all the people who don't, or all the store owners and office managers who also don't have the time to care for their indoor plants. As a plant consultant, that green thumb of yours can make a very rewarding business—in every sense of the word.

WHO HIRES CONSULTANTS?

The history of consulting may be as old as civilization itself. When humans discovered how to produce more food than their families needed, some among them figured out how to sell the excess to other families, and, in a way, they became the first consultants. As fewer people were needed to produce food, more people concentrated on building civilizations, and by sharing their ideas and their skills, they created what we still call progress. If they had kept those skills to themselves and not spent some of their time consulting, we may never have left the Stone Age.

Sharing information is a well-established tradition, and in our age it has become a booming business. Society is getting more complex, and the need for consultants increases every day. People are more willing to admit they don't have all the answers and recognize the need for asking more questions. As a specialist who knows the right answers or knows where to find them, you are going to find your services very much in demand.

ACCENTUATE THE POSITIVE

In your search for information about becoming a consultant, you may already have come across some books and articles that compare the profession to witch doctors and worse. Consultant-bashing was fashionable in the media a couple of years ago. Even Dilbert milked a few laughs from the profession.

But all that has changed. A few companies that routinely used consultants decided that going it alone was probably the politically correct thing to do and changed their policies. It didn't take long for most of them to realize they had made a mistake. It turned out to be a case of throwing out the baby with the bath, and the wave of consultant-bashing may well have resulted in a boost for you. Many companies that experimented with banning consultants have since seen the light, and most have found that using consultants wasn't the problem, it was using the wrong ones. They discovered that the bad press consultants received was sometimes justified, such as in the cases of large consulting firms that offer general solutions to specific problems. The obvious solution, they've found, is to look for help from smaller consulting practices, ones that are better able to concentrate on their specific and unique needs—businesses like the one you are contemplating.

Very few savvy businesspeople consider it a luxury to hire consultants anymore and most consider it the only way to keep ahead. And this attitude extends beyond the business world. Government agencies and nonprofit organizations regularly turn to consultants, not just to keep their information flow up to date, but to help keep their fixed costs in line. Individuals, especially families where both partners are building careers, are also hungry for the help of consultants to deal with all kinds of problems—from finding the right schools for their children to dressing for success and dealing with success through financial planning.

Nobody feels quite able to go it alone in today's complicated world, either in aspects of their careers or in their personal lives, and that's where you come in. As a consultant you'll be part teacher, part Dutch uncle, part trusted friend. You'll be putting your knowledge and experience where it will do the most good, and nothing could be more satisfying than that.

DO YOU HAVE WHAT IT TAKES?

It isn't likely that taking an aptitude test is one of the things you were planning to do before becoming a consultant. You're probably going to base your decision on your own past experience and your ability to find clients among companies or individuals who can benefit from it. But some factors are measurable, and one large consulting organization, the Human Engineering Laboratory of the Johnson O'Connor Research Foundation, has been doing it since 1922. Every set of tests it gives at fourteen locations around the country is compared to more than 300,000 other tests and the career paths of people who have taken them. What they've discovered provides valuable insight on a person's aptitudes for things that can make a difference. Since your goal right now is planning for a second life, where you've been up until now is going to be an important part of your plan. You already know what your professional strengths are, and you're aware of your weaknesses, too, but some of the things the Foundation has discovered might help you understand the things that make you unique.

Among the areas it explores is what the testers call "graphoria," the ability to check things quickly and accurately, measured by the timed grouping of columns of numbers. Such a skill is indispensable to most consulting practices, which require absorbing information from a client before making recommendations. But before you say, "Anybody can do that," you should know that not everyone has that skill. According to the research, it turns out that women are as much as 75 percent more likely to have an aptitude for speed and accuracy in checking information than men who have taken the test.

The ability to come up with new ideas is obviously central to a successful consultancy and the researchers at the Human Engineering Laboratory have found that people who have a strong aptitude for this thing they label "ideaphoria" are likely to change jobs a lot because they need more creative challenge than any single job can give them. If that has been your experience, and you consider yourself a strong idea person, you're surely on the right track in becoming a consultant. Remember when potential employers sneered at your résumé because you had bounced from job to job too many times? As a consultant you're going to find that to be an asset.

The patterns the tests have revealed suggest that one of the keys to success in running a small business is the ability to concentrate on long-range goals. Another desirable quality, especially among consultants, is inductive reasoning, the ability to see relationships in what ordinarily appear to be unrelated ideas and information. The researchers have noted that people who score low in this area usually have a lot of patience, which is an asset for a consultant, but it is generally coupled with an accepting nature, which can be a liability. High scorers, on the other hand, have instincts that guarantee success in any profession, especially consulting.

A great deal of the work you'll do as a consultant will involve writing proposals and reports, and it goes without saying that a large vocabulary is a great asset. If you're planning to become a management consultant, the research suggests it is vital. After all these years of testing, Johnson O'Connor has found that the highest vocabulary scores are routinely racked up by business executives who consistently beat professional editors and writers in word power. The tests have also revealed something else: while a high vocabulary doesn't guarantee success in any field, a low one almost always leads to failure.

But when all these things are weighed in the balance, the testers say that understanding your aptitudes is only part of your blueprint for the future. Another of the tests Johnson O'Connor gives measures personality and separates "objective" traits from "subjective" ones. Everybody's makeup, they say, is based on one or the other but never a combination of the two. Their research finds that three out of every four people have objective personalities— that is, their outlook on life generally takes a broad view, and they tend to accept the input of others. They are more likely to react to problems from an external point of view rather than through inner thoughts or personal feelings. If you are in that category, chances are quite good that you'll do well as a consultant.

On the other hand, if you have a subjective personality, you are more likely to look at life from a personal point of view. You are what fortune-tellers call "a deep thinker," and while that can be an asset in some kinds of consulting, you're going to need to be careful in your approach to your business. Subjective people are more likely to be individualists with an ability to focus on a problem for as long as it takes to work it out, but they actually prefer working alone and it annoys them to have anyone else involved in their work.

If you have a subjective personality, it may be what's drawing you to life on your own, but beware—subjective people don't often have much patience with other people's points of view about their work, not even their spouses'. Consulting is a people-oriented business, a two-way street where the client's ideas are important, too. If you're too dogmatic about your own concepts and don't like accepting opinions as well as offering them, you're probably going to be doomed from the start.

A NEW LIFE

You know that you have the aptitudes to become a consultant and the personality to make it a happy choice, but what if the work you're currently doing has nothing to do with the field you're dreaming about. Suppose that you've been selling real estate but you'd really rather decorate houses than sell them.

The Johnson O'Connor researchers say that unused aptitudes are invariably what's at the root of most career crises. If you've been making use of some, but not all, of your abilities through your working life, they believe, the abilities you've neglected will assert themselves at some point and you'll find your outlook changing. For instance, if you've discovered that you have a talent for fund-raising, but you've built your career around your ability as a manager in the corporate world, chances are you'll eventually find management unfulfilling. That's when you'll be volunteering to serve on committees for nonprofit organizations and the job that pays your salary begins to pale by comparison. At this point it's probably time for you to consider a second career as a consultant for those nonprofits and let them pay you instead.

Of course, in the majority of consultancies experience counts most of all, and what you'll be selling in your new life is the expertise you built up in your old one. But don't overlook facets of your past experience or your special interests that can be applied to new situations.

Having said that, the next question is, How do you go about doing it? Terms like "hard work," "tenacity," and "determination" come to mind. And they are all important. But ask a consultant what it takes and a word you'll often hear is "luck"—not the kind of luck that helps you win the lottery, but the kind that comes from recognizing opportunities when they come along and then doing something about them. It's the kind of luck you make for yourself; it's a game anybody can win. It all begins with making a decision to change your life, and, with it, your luck.

CREATING YOUR OWN WORLD

Your past experience is the guiding factor to success as a consultant, but, quite often, succeeding in a job is the very thing that leads to the decision to go off on your own. You may have discovered that success wasn't everything you expected it to be. When you do, it may be a signal to create your own world and find success on your own terms.

A great many successful business executives say they'd be happier if they could still be doing the things that led to their success in the first place. A salesperson who built friendly relationships with clients and then lost touch with them as a sales manager may miss the good old days, even if today's paycheck is much bigger. A person who climbed the corporate ladder may look back at a time when work was more fun with fewer meetings and less responsibility and wonder if the climb was worth it. Yes, there is more money and more prestige at the top, but often that prestige can be a key to a successful career as an independent consultant, and chances are the money will follow. Best of all, when you're on your own, you can be flexible enough to create the kind of opportunities that you want to pursue.

BEATING THE CLOCK

One of the biggest problems most consultants face is balancing their time. When you establish your consultancy, perhaps as much as a quarter of your time will be spent working on your marketing plan and looking for new business. And then when the new business comes in, you are going to need to concentrate on your clients' needs. But that's not all. At the core of every consultancy is a pressing need to stay educated about developments in your field. This holds true in every field, whether you're a nutritionist, a personal trainer, or a tax consultant. And that means doing a huge amount of reading of anything related to your speciality. You will also need to network with other consultants, so you can tap into what they've learned and share the things you've learned yourself. In the consulting business, nothing is more important than knowledge. You just can't get enough of it.

Being on the cutting edge is particularly critical in the world of computer consultants. Although most pride themselves on being on top of fast-changing developments in their field, many find there is also a solid market for the deep background they've aquired in technology they themselves may consider old-hat. Most companies can't afford to keep up with every change that comes along, and so they do everything they can to keep their old hardware and software producing the results they need. As the millennium approaches, more and more computer consultants are making more money than they ever dreamed possible as companies and government agencies beg for help in solving the year 2000 problem built into their computer systems.

WORKING ON THE CLIENT'S PREMISES

In many different kinds of consultancies, working on the client's premises is standard procedure, and often the best way to get the job done. This is largely true among management consultants, but for computer and data processing experts it is usually the only way.

The computer industry grew so fast and it changes so often that it has been virtually impossible for developers of hardware and software to find qualified employees quickly enough. Typically, it takes up to two months for any company to fill an open job, and in an industry whose lifeblood is change, that simply isn't acceptable. The obvious answer is to use consultants, and over the years it has become a standard practice for such professionals to work on-site for a single client. There are thousands of programmers and systems analysts, systems designers and systems engineers who work for themselves but have spent years going to someone else's office every day. Some work in the computer industry itself, many work for corporations that use the technology, and others work for government agencies.

BE SURE TO BE TRULY INDEPENDENT

There is one government agency that looks at all this with a jaundiced eye, the Internal Revenue Service. Although the hiring of consultants has become as common as full-time staffing in dealing with technology, the contracts are nearly always long-term and always require on-site work. Does that mean these consultants are really employees? In many cases, the IRS says "absolutely." Companies usually label consultants "independent contractors," but the tax people have their own ideas about what that means.

If you are planning to establish your consulting practice working exclusively for your former employer, for instance, you'd better think twice before you do it. Suppose your company offers you a chance to take early retirement with a generous buyout and an opportunity to start collecting pension benefits long before you're sixty-five. Such a thing, as they say, may be an offer you can't refuse. But then suppose the company asks you to come back a couple of days a week as a consultant. What could be better? You'd be collecting a pension, you'd be free to invest all that money you collected in the buyout, and you'd still be getting a paycheck. Don't even think about it. The tax collector won't allow it. Anyone who leaves a company with a golden parachute is forbidden by IRS regulations to go on collecting money from that company, and that includes consulting fees. No matter how attractive such an opportunity may seem, if you do sign on as a consultant after taking a buyout, chances are good that you'll be audited and not only have to pay back taxes but big fines as well.

In addition, your former employer will have to pay fines, too, no matter how innocent the arrangement may have been.

BE AWARE OF THE RULES

When you start your consulting business, it makes good sense to make former employers your clients. You know their business, their policies, and their problems and your input will probably be welcome, but take note of the ways the IRS separates independent contractors from employees:

- If you work for just one client, the tax people may not believe you are running your own business.
- If your consultancy contract forbids working for a company's competitor, the IRS won't believe you're not an employee.
- If you go back to help a former employer and do all your work out of the old office with the company's equipment and facilities, the tax people will think nothing else has changed either.
- If you claim to be an independent businessperson, you need to be able to back it up with proof that you've made a financial investment in your business.
- If you are providing input that is key to running someone else's business rather than just helping to make it better, chances are that will raise a red flag at the tax office.

The same tests apply to all consultants who work for extended periods of time on-site for a single client, even if they never were regular employees. In the early 1990s, the IRS began telling big companies with independent contractors under their roof that these people were actually "common-law employees," and that millions in taxes and interest was long overdue. The companies responded with a definition of their own and began calling them "temps," which created a bonanza for temporary agencies that took on the responsibility of making them their employees. But the jury is still out, literally, as a case against Microsoft and its use of long-term temporary help grinds its way toward the Supreme Court.

AN ALTERNATIVE TO YOUR OWN BUSINESS

The outcome of that case may change all the rules, but in the meantime, the Alexandria, Virginia–based National Association of Temporary Services says that more than 1,100 temporary-help companies are filling more than a million job assignments every day.

When you think of temporaries, clerks and typists and security guards come to mind, but the fact is that those million jobs a day are more likely being filled by consultants. And there are some advantages in the arrangement. For one thing, working as a temporary means that you don't have to market yourself, and it means that you can work as little or as much as you choose. As an employee of a temporary agency, you get a regular paycheck, thereby paying taxes as you go along. It is a wonderful opportunity for a retired person who still wants to keep active but would rather not be bothered establishing and running their own business.

Right now, there are more than 6.5 million people working as temporaries, and collectively they are earning more than $10 billion a year. Not all are receptionists and secretaries. Many are engineers, lawyers, writers, designers, and other professionals. Some function as chief executive officers, chief financial officers, and other executive-suite types known in the trade as "interim executives."

The big advantage of working for a temporary agency is that it leaves you free to use all your time earning money rather than losing billable hours to marketing and running your business. It also gives you freedom from commitment. If you find an assignment that isn't what you expected, it is easy to walk away from it and into another that's a better fit. Temping also allows you to explore new fields with less risk, and, in many cases, it allows you to travel to new places as agencies find assignments beyond your normal horizon.

It is true that you'll be able to earn more as an independent consultant without a middleman dipping into your pockets, but it is also true that temporary agencies have more experience at negotiating fees than you might, and it is quite likely that you'll come out ahead. The bottom line, either way, is that as a consultant you can earn up to twice as much as an employee doing the same job. Obviously, as a consultant you won't qualify for fringe benefits, but the higher income can often offset that many times over.

Some consultants work both sides of the street, often beginning their practice working for a temporary agency or for a large consulting firm. Over time, they hone their skills and develop new contacts before hanging out their own shingle. And many regard temping as an ace in the hole when their independent business slows.

Of course, many others regard working for a temporary agency as a sure way to give up the freedom and independence they were looking for in the first place. However, as a backstop to a consulting career or a relatively risk-free way to start one, it is well worth exploring.

Exploration is easy. Most temporary agencies spell out their specialties in Yellow Pages advertising and in newspaper classifieds. Once you've located the ones whose specialties match yours, simply send them each a résumé, just as though you were looking for a regular job. It would help to call them, too, to separate yourself from the rest of the pack, but in general that is all the marketing you'll have to do.

THE SPICE OF LIFE

Most consultants begin their independent careers in the same field that previously brought them steady paychecks. For the most part, they leverage their life experience to take advantage of new opportunities and to find new challenges, but once they escape the confines of a regular job, even those who picked up where they left off when they decided to become their own boss usually discover new interests, new needs, and new ways of doing things. It goes with the territory. When you become a consultant, no experience you've ever had is wasted, no interest needs to be unfulfilled. The key word is variety, something that is missing from too many nine-to-five jobs. As a consultant, every assignment is a learning opportunity. And everything you learn represents a chance to offer something new. Can you think of a better way to find satisfaction in your own life and earn a living while you're at it?

CHAPTER THREE

A Day in the Life of a Freelance Consultant

The prospect of not having a boss interrupting your train of thought every five minutes may be one of the reasons you're hoping to be on your own one day, but don't think there won't be interruptions you didn't plan for, and days without enough hours to get everything done. No more than there is a typical consultant, will there be a "typical" day in your life when you become one—except that most of them will be long and many will be hectic.

When you begin working for yourself, your routine will best be determined by your own natural rhythms. Some people find they work best late at night, others believe they accomplish more at the crack of dawn. Either way, unless you will be working on-site for your clients, you won't be living in a nine-to-five world anymore. Although you'll need to be bright-eyed and bushy-tailed for interacting with your clients during their regular business day, you will be free to handle problem-solving at times when you feel most productive.

However, that doesn't mean you can put off handling the details of your consultancy until you "feel like it." Self-discipline is the key to success in running any small business, and for a consultant it is crucial. Set up a routine for yourself and try not to vary from it unless it is unavoidable. The nature of your consulting practice will get you all the variety you could wish for, and it will keep your routine from becoming mundane.

But what is "routine" in the life of a consultant? A few of the consultants interviewed for this book agreed to describe a day in their working life selected at random, in their own way and in their own words. The days they chose may not be typical of their overall work patterns, nor of yours when you go into business for yourself, but together they'll give you some clues about what might lie ahead.

VICKIE SHERMAN—Human Dynamics, Johnson City, TN

After working for twenty years in human resources on the corporate level, Vickie formed her own independent consultancy a few years ago because, as she puts it, "I wanted to be in control of my own future."

Rather than describing a typical day in my life as a consultant, I think it would be more helpful to do an overview of the ups and downs of life in general now that I am on my own.

You certainly cannot sit around and wait for people to seek out your wisdom. I spend as much of my day as possible on the phone setting up appointments or actually sitting in front of people keeping those appointments. I have to force this behavior because it is outside my "comfort zone." I suffer from call reluctance because as a former corporate person I was always extremely busy and did not appreciate being interrupted by "sales calls." However, if it were not for those occasional solicitations, I would not have had knowledge of the services available to me.

I belong to a networking group and keep trying to perfect my skills. I have found "partnering" to be an excellent sales tool. Specifically, that is piggybacking with other service providers who deal with the same client base. I work with temporary staffing agencies to get an introduction to a client company that seems to be having ongoing problems with turnover, absenteeism, complaints about "bad management" and so forth. The temp agency is already in the business on an almost daily basis and has rapport. It is easy for them to introduce me, and in doing so, it enhances their perceived value to the client since they are truly partnering for solutions to business problems. I would always rather have an introduction than go in on a cold call.

It is hard to stay "up" sometimes. You get really busy putting together a lot of great proposals for projects you would really like to work on, and it drags on and on. You end up getting discouraged. I have learned to put presentations together with gusto and then put them out of my mind except for regular follow-up calls. That way, I don"t get my hopes up too much. I've learned never to count on a contract until it is signed and you have actually started the work. Anything can happen. My goals are like pouring things into the top of a huge funnel. If you pour enough into the top, a few are going to come out the bottom. I never let the pipeline dry up, no matter how promising a job might look. It takes a long time to get the pipeline churning again, and you could starve before it does.

The most heartwarming thing that has happened to me since I went out on my own is that I have made a lot of great new friends and acquaintances who might not have entered my circle except through my networking activities. They include people in business, education, industry, entrepreneurs, and others. It's funny, we really support one another on those bad days. To the rest of the world, we are always doing JUST GREAT!

The most awful thing that has happened to me since I started my business is that I received a phone call from a large physician's group that was combining seven private practices into one facility and wanted customer service training. I spent two weeks observing each of the practices, I bought current books on customer service and made copious notes as I read them. I wrote the first twenty-five pages of a detailed training manual and then attempted to set an appointment to review my progress and set aside dates for the actual training to take place. I quickly discovered that they had decided to cancel the project because they had not gotten the approval of all the physicians to spend the money for the program.

The bottom line is that although I billed them $10,000, it was never paid. I chose to chalk it up to experience. Even though I was assured I could collect if I pursued it legally, it would cost me money to do so. Lesson learned? Make sure every person scheduling your work has the authority to do so. Even an informal contract is better than no contract. In the meantime, I have a dynamite customized program for medical practice customer service.

MICHAEL NELSON—The Solution Consortium, Bloomington, MN
Michael is a management consultant whose company specializes in long-range planning, problem-solving, and human resources issues for clients as diverse as restaurants and law firms.

Due to my own idiosyncracies, I make a list every day so that I know at the end I will have accomplished what I set out to do. So often in the past, I would have such great intentions each morning, only to reach the end of the day frustrated that I had just picked at several projects instead of completing anything concrete. Keep in mind that I am a morning person in the extreme. My wife, Kathy, who has trouble looking 9 A.M. squarely in the face, doesn't understand.

5A.M. Wake, stretch, shave, make coffee, retrieve the papers and meditate if I'm so inclined.

5:30A.M. Peruse Day Timer; review yesterday and make a list of what to accomplish today, checking that list against current projects and goals to make sure each thing is getting some attention. Copy a brief version of the list onto a card for my pocket reference.

6A.M. Cell phone on. Check and respond to E-mail and several consultant and human resources bulletin boards online.

6:30A.M. Perhaps breakfast and read the local paper, especially the business pages and the front page. Opportunities abound in stories of local companies on the rise.

7A.M. Into the shower, wake the wife, finish the local paper (never skip the comics, they're very important to a balanced day). Drive Kathy to work.

8A.M. Either drive to meetings, returning phone calls on the way, or stop for coffee and read *The Wall Street Journal*. This is when I usually stop in at clients' offices to inform them of yesterday's results, if any, and catch up on necessary information. Working from home is great, but person-to-person contact leaves a lasting impression on a client. AND, it relieves them of any anxiety they may have, even if the visit is only for a few minutes.

9A.M. Begin attacking the list, whether it be meetings, document preparation, returning phone calls, administering web pages, writing or researching for clients, cold calls, writing or researching for my own seminars or articles, maintaining calendars, inputting financial records, billing, or whatever else needs to be done. I make sure that everything I need to get done is on the card in my pocket. It is amazing how often something I thought might take an hour only takes fifteen minutes—and that time-saving is instantly realized as I check off the items. The only set times in my daily block, from nine to five, are for scheduled meetings and phone calls. That allows me not to worry about how long an item takes. It just gets done without any hassles.

11:30A.M. Seven days out of ten, a small bucket of balls at the driving range fits nicely here.

NOON Lunch somewhere with a client or a prospect or alone someplace where I'm a regular that caters to others who may be able to utilize my services some day.

1P.M. Back to the list. If, like me, your office is your cell phone and your laptop, please, please, please use this time out on your deck, by a pool, or anywhere that your mind can be free and comfortable. I firmly believe that being a really good consultant requires creativity to be able to provide the solutions clients are counting on but that they don't believe they can produce by themselves. We owe it to our clients to be clear-headed and open-minded. Otherwise they could have hired another drone to sit under fluorescent lights all day grinding out the same tired responses. There are usually at least three cell phones in operation around the pool in our condominium complex at any given time. We're all doing business, but we're also able to smile and jump into the pool when the sun's too hot.

4P.M. Begin to think about picking up Kathy from work. Retry unsuccessful phone calls during the drive.

5:30P.M. Figure out what's for dinner, cook and eat. Some days I begin cooking in the afternoon, do laundry or leisure reading earlier in the early afternoon if my morning was efficient.

6 P.M. Cell phone off. Know when to say "when." If it's an emergency, they'll find you.

7:30P.M. Reading, Internet research, or family time.

10:30P.M. Make sure all the day's activities have been documented in my Day Timer and are ready to go when I get up tomorrow morning. This closure makes me absolutely able to forget about work entirely while I sleep.

11P.M. Leisure reading. Work-related reading is forbidden after the Day Timer has been updated. Meditate if I'm so inclined.

Because I take thirty minutes every morning to organize my day, I'm usually finished with all business-related items by 2 in the afternoon. That leaves me with plenty of time to do things I enjoy, like reading and puttering around the house. I deliberately try to schedule meetings in the morning when I'm fresh and can make a better impression. When a client needs to meet late in the afternoon, I don't eat lunch and thereby avoid the lethargy it creates.

When you have a goal and work backwards from the realization of that goal, mapping out everything you need to do to achieve it, nothing can stop you. Nothing, that is, if you spend part of every day working toward that goal. It's very simple when you follow a plan. That bit of advice allows me to achieve extraordinary results for companies in strategic distress. They can be told a million times, but until they actually do it, or have someone force them to do it, they just aren't ready for success. The secret is simple: Love greatly. Think clearly. Live deeply.

BETSY PETERS—Slice of New York, New York, NY
Betsy's company is a type of consultancy known in the travel trade as a "ground operator." She consults with organizations

and corporations holding conventions and meetings in New York to provide tours, meeting and party sites, and other services.

My day began with an 8 A.M. presentation to the spouses of attendees at a sales conference. Most of these people don't know much about New York except what they see on *Law and Order* or *NYPD Blue*, and my job is to assure them that nothing but an enjoyable time is in store for them. We have organized six different tours for them to choose from, and this breakfast meeting is the time to sell them. Some will spend the day shopping, others will go backstage at a theater and then see the show, and some will opt for sightseeing.

After the meeting, I need to make sure that all the buses are outside the hotel and that all my guides are on deck. It turns out that the girl who was going to do the theater trip didn't show up and I decide to handle it myself. The bus isn't scheduled to leave for another hour and that gives me time to run over to the office to make sure there are no other problems.

Our office is near the tourist hotels and the theater district, which is not only convenient for client presentations, but allows us to turn on a dime when things go wrong. I have three people working there and each of them knows every aspect of the business. On this day, though, things seem to be going smoothly, and I am able to use the hour to reconfirm sites and guide service for events scheduled for the rest of this weeklong meeting. The company we're serving is in the pharmaceuticals business and we have arranged to bus all five hundred of the meeting attendees out to its corporate headquarters in New Jersey for a tour later in the week. It will require a fleet of buses, all leaving the city in the middle of the rush hour. I take the time to check with the bus company to make sure we're up to the challenge.

The theater tour begins with a luncheon, and although the hotel, the restaurant, and the theater are all within about four blocks of each other, we move the people from one to the other by bus. I get back to the hotel in plenty of time to catch the bus, grateful for the greeters we've stationed at the hotel to take care of our spouses. During lunch, I do a lot of table-hopping to make sure everyone is pleased with our service so far and, coincidentally, to recommend other tours we're providing for them.

I have seen this show one time too many, but I go with them for the backstage tour and then leave before curtain time to run back to the office. We have just signed a contract to handle an upcoming convention of the Congressional Medal of Honor Society, and there is a lot of work to be done.

Among other things involved is finding a headquarters hotel. A highlight of the convention will be a luncheon attended by the President of the United States. Not every hotel is able to handle that, and I've already checked out all the ones that can. My final choice is the Sheraton, but I need to put my reasons in writing to convince the committee.

I arrived back at the theater to a round of applause at the final curtain, and smilingly load my people into the bus for the two-block ride back to their hotel. As for myself, I opt for walking and I'm there long before the bus is.

We have a catered dinner party planned for tonight at an old opera house I discovered out in Brooklyn. It is scheduled to begin at 8, but I am there by 6:30, in time to greet the florist who has turned the place into a veritable garden. We have hired entertainers, too, and I use my cell phone to contact them. Thankfully, they are on their way. I have also hired an ambulance service because of the size of the group and the remoteness of the venue. The ambulance is there, but it is parked at the front door. That will never do. The driver and I do a quick walking tour of the neighborhood to find a more discrete parking spot.

Our guests are safely back at the hotel by midnight, and several are interested in doing some exploring on their own. I make suggestions and send them on their way, wondering how in the world they are going to be in shape for tomorrow's meetings.

I need to be upbeat tomorrow myself. We have a 9 A.M. meeting with an association president who is planning a conference with fifteen hundred attendees. It is important to me that he'll put my company at the heart of his plan. I'm confident that he will, but just for insurance, I stop by the office to go over my presentation one more time.

MARYANN FRIEDLANDER—Cleveland, OH

MaryAnn is a marketing research consultant whose practice ranges from establishing marketing strategies for existing companies to analyzing markets for start-up companies. Among her assignments have been researching the feasibility of building an ice-skating rink in Florida and defining the market for a would-be ostrich farmer.

I have two different types of days, those that involve working on a project and those I spend soliciting business. Both are equally important.

On "Project Days" where a deadline is involved, I block out the time in advance on my calendar and do not overbook my time. On these days, I wake up at about 8 A.M. and go straight to my computer. I eat breakfast while analyzing and typing in my home office. I let my messages go into my phone mail during the morning so I can concentrate. I will break at midmorning and go into the Internet and read my E-mail. Depending on my progress on the project, I will spend anywhere from five to thirty minutes online reading or answering my mail. Lunch is usually something quick and easy. If I have an errand to run or phone calls to make, I will go out for an hour or so in the afternoon. At a minimum, I try to take a sanity break for at least an hour in the afternoon, and will work up until dinner. I always go back to a job after dinner, either to finish it up or proofread it until about 10. My schedule the next day begins according to how much I have accomplished during this day. If I have enough time before a meeting to finish the project, sometimes I'll leave it until morning so I can get enough sleep. Unfortunately, most projects take far longer than I expect, so many nights I don't finish up before midnight.

On "Selling Days," when I need to do my phone work, I wake up a little more leisurely and usually start on the telephone at about 9:30. I spend time on my computer looking through sources and directories that I think will have potential leads. I take the time to call and verify my leads before I actually send out sales information to them. I also telephone potential leads that I have already sent information to, and follow up to schedule meetings with them.

Sometimes I use these days to schedule project meetings or presentations with clients, or I call other business owners or professional friends and go to lunch or have coffee with them.

I try to take advantage of less busy days cleaning up or getting organized. I spend time on the Internet doing extra research and sometimes I spend extra time at the library or catching up with my trade journals and business books. Even if I am not working on a project, I spend my days focused on new ways to grow my business.

CHAPTER FOUR

Thinking It Through

Vickie Sherman, a human resources consultant based in Johnson City, Tennessee, worked for more than twenty years for a variety of companies both large and small, union and non-union, domestic and international before becoming Vice President of Human Resources for a multinational company. After reaching that level, she decided that she didn't want to stay there for the next twenty years. "There was no challenge," she says. "I'm a results-oriented person, not a 'maintenance' person."

"I wanted to be in control of my future," she adds, "and I knew there is certainly no security in corporate America." The obvious answer was to become an independent consultant, but Vickie didn't just hand in her resignation. "I drafted a proposal to eliminate my own position as a cost-saving measure, thus making me eligible for severance pay," she confesses. "The proposal was accepted, and I was free to go off on my own."

MaryAnn Friedlander had specialized in consumer research for a large corporation and for several different advertising agencies for a dozen years before a Cleveland-based company offered her a retainer to help their marketing department develop new strategies. It meant giving up the security of a regular job, but she had always found the corporate environment constraining and the offer represented an opportunity for freedom. She has since used that freedom to expand her horizons and her skills evolved into marketing research, which she has found valuable to small companies interested in maintaining growth in a changing environment.

Are MaryAnn and Vickie typical consultants? They are in terms of the business they've built for themselves, even if they started them in different ways. Both of them, like most other consultants, used the work experience they gained employed by someone else to create a new business of their own, and both have added to their success by building on their experiences. A successful consultancy usually stems from what a consultant brings to the table in terms of past experience, contacts within an industry, and most of all, an attitude that says, "I'm here to help you."

When Jim McClure was downsized out of a telecommunications company, he knew that his twenty-eight years of experience was valuable. He wasn't eligible for retirement benefits, but Jim didn't believe he was ready to retire anyway. He was having too much fun. His old job had involved handling corporate public relations, and he knew that there were plenty of companies in the Chicago area where he lives who could use the help of a man with his experience. Once having found them, he began marketing himself as a PR writer, but he quickly realized that he had much more to offer than just writing skills. He does a lot of sales training these days, and because of his years of experience in a union environment, he is in demand among companies that need crisis control when they're faced with labor problems. "It's become a lost art," he says, "and many corporate PR people don't know how to communicate with the public when they have labor problems." Fortunately, Jim hasn't forgotten the art.

LOOK BEFORE YOU LEAP

The decision to go from the security of a regular job or, as in Jim's case, a comfortable retirement, to the uncertainty of striking out on your own should begin with an honest look at what you have to offer. Analyze your strengths, your weaknesses, your past experiences, and your talents. Take a personal inventory of what works for you and what doesn't, and think about what you expect from the future.

Working as a consultant, no matter what your specialty, requires an enormous amount of self-discipline. You'll need to be able to deal with deadlines, either the ones you set for yourself or the ones your clients will demand. And you'll need to push yourself to keep on working whether you like it or not. One of the most frequently cited reasons people give for wanting to go into business for themselves is "to be on my own." But as a consultant, you are never really on your own. By definition, you will be helping other people work their way through their problems or plans. That means, first and foremost, that you'll have to be a patient listener. And you're going to have to be able to keep your opinions to yourself until you've thought them through, too.

Still, you are going to be on your own in a different sense. You'll be making a living through your own talents without a guaranteed paycheck, health benefits, and security. More often than not, you'll finish an assignment and be out of work until you find the next one. Like everything else, consulting has a downside. But as long as you're prepared for them, the roadblocks you encounter won't necessarily be problems you can't handle.

EXPLORE THE MARKET

No matter how they arrived at the decision to become independent consultants, by and large, most never seem to have given a second thought to "the competition." In most types of consultancy, professionals regularly call on what in any other kind of business would be called "competitors" to help get assignments completed. In most cases, they are called "associates," and that's a reflection on the nature of a consultant practice.

If you were opening a retail store or establishing a restaurant, it is undeniable that you'd need to make sure you have a competitive edge before you start, but consultancy is a very personal business, and no matter how many other people in your area have the same speciality, none of them will approach a problem in quite the same way. The business of consulting is more closely related to custom cabinet-making or designing sailboats than running a restaurant or bringing customers into your retail store.

But even cabinetmakers and sailboat designers need to look around them before they begin selling their services. They need to know where their markets are, who else is in that market, and how difficult it is going to be to become established.

PLAN FOR SUCCESS

Sometimes it may seem that it isn't important to have a business plan to start a consultancy practice. It's often a field that changes with the times and opportunities are frequently unexpected. You may have a gut feeling that your background and your personality practically guarantee success, and since it doesn't take a lot of money to get started, it may seem easier to just go ahead and wing it. Of course you can, but it just isn't a good idea.

It's quite possible that you can make it as a consultant on your unique experience alone, but if you you hope to be secure doing it, you need to think of consulting as a business as much as it is a fulfilling profession. Keep in mind that once you're on your own, fulfillment also means supporting yourself and your family.

ASK THE EXPERTS

If you're like most people contemplating becoming a full-time consultant, your number-one goal is independence. It's an important one, but no matter how independent you expect to be, you'll never be completely free of the rules and regulations that affect every small business, even the ones you're not aware of.

What would it be worth for you to know ahead of time about the things that could haunt you after you start your business? How does free expert advice sound? Right now, just around the corner and waiting for your call is a retired executive who wants to share the experiences of a lifetime with you—a consultant, if you will; but this consultant is working for nothing more than the joy of it and you won't get a bill for the service.

An agency of the Small Business Administration called the Service Corps of Retired Executives (SCORE for short) specializes in helping people like you who want to be on their own. These volunteers can tell you just about everything you need to know about starting up a new business and keeping it alive. One of them will know exactly how to put a business plan together and how local, state, and federal laws will affect your new venture. And, again, the consultation won't cost you a dime.

You'll find the nearest SCORE office listed under "US Government" in the telephone book, along with the various numbers for the Small Business Administration. You'll also find the agency on the Internet under the keyword SBA. All of its services are free and they're all designed to help you make your business work.

SCORE has more than three hundred offices around the country, staffed by more than three thousand volunteers, all of whom are seasoned business veterans. It isn't likely that you'll need their help with your specific area of expertise, but there are basic rules that apply to every small business and SCORE's volunteers are on hand every day to show you how those rules can affect yours.

As a consultant, you're an idea person, but unless your practice is in areas like financial planning or management consulting, you may find financial details difficult, even boring. However, it goes without saying that when you're in business for yourself, keeping an eye on your money is a matter of life and death. The people at SCORE can help you simplify the financial aspects of your business, not just at the beginning but down the road as well. In terms of your initial start-up investment, most of the rules that apply to other small businesses probably won't apply to yours because in most types of consultancies you can get up and running on a shoestring budget. Still, there is an investment required even if it is a small one. You may need a more sophisticated computer and new software, for instance, as well as office supplies and furnishings for your new office.

Most accountants, and probably the people at SCORE too, will advise you to have as much in savings as it will cost you to live for six months to a year. It is solid advice and you should take it seriously. But you'd be suprised how many people don't. Lisa Kirazian, who works with nonprofit organizations in the Los Angeles area to help them select funding sources and to write grant proposals, is someone you'd expect to plan for her own financial needs months in advance. But she admits she doesn't. "I spend money too fast," she confesses, "and I just concentrate on making it as I go along." Her attitude is a reflection of a personality trait that's valuable to a consultant: confidence. It may be an admirable quality, and it is certainly one of the keys to success as a consultant. But wouldn't you really rather not have to worry about money when you're finding solutions to a client's problems? And, even more important, wouldn't it be great to be able to turn down assignments you'd rather not bother with?

IS THIS BUSINESS RIGHT FOR YOU?

Finding success as a consultant has less to do with your experience, or even your personality, than with your attitude. You may consider yourself an entrepreneurial type and that surely is an asset when you go into business for yourself. But things like self-discipline and organization, attention to detail, dealing with people, and occasionally doing things you may not enjoy are what will determine your success.

Try the following questionnaire written by Charles L. Sodikoff, Ph.D., a psychologist and career management professional who has counseled people like you for the last fifteen years. It will add to your understanding of whether you have the ability and willingness to go off on your own.

PROFILE FOR SUCCESS

Take a minute to circle the numbers that apply to you:

Ability to Do
4 = Real strength
3 = Able to do
2 = Need to work on
1 = Real weakness

Willingness to Do
4 = Really like doing
3 = Not a problem
2 = Do not want to do
1 = Will not do

	Ability to Do	Willingness to Do
Managing your own time	4 3 2 1	4 3 2 1
Organizing your day	4 3 2 1	4 3 2 1
Working long hours	4 3 2 1	4 3 2 1
Working on weekends	4 3 2 1	4 3 2 1

	Ability to Do	Willingess to Do
Putting personal and family plans on hold	4 3 2 I	4 3 2 I
Meeting people/talking to strangers	4 3 2 I	4 3 2 I
Mixing business and social activities	4 3 2 I	4 3 2 I
Selling yourself to others	4 3 2 I	4 3 2 I
Selling products or services	4 3 2 I	4 3 2 I
Working with demanding or difficult customers/ clients	4 3 2 I	4 3 2 I
Respecting other people's opinions	4 3 2 I	4 3 2 I
Changing your ideas even if they're perfect	4 3 2 I	4 3 2 I
Working on own without others to share ideas	4 3 2 I	4 3 2 I
Setting long-range goals and specific targets	4 3 2 I	4 3 2 I
Taking a planned and organized approach to your work	4 3 2 I	4 3 2 I
Juggling multiple jobs at one time	4 3 2 I	4 3 2 I
Doing clerical tasks	4 3 2 I	4 3 2 I
Working under tight deadlines	4 3 2 I	4 3 2 I
Looking for creative solutions to problems	4 3 2 I	4 3 2 I
Making difficult decisions	4 3 2 I	4 3 2 I
Solving problems on the spot	4 3 2 I	4 3 2 I

	Ability to Do	Willingess to Do
Dealing with uncertainty	4 3 2 1	4 3 2 1
Having patience to "stick-with-it" through slow periods	4 3 2 1	4 3 2 1
Investing your own money	4 3 2 1	4 3 2 1
Understanding and maintaining financial records	4 3 2 1	4 3 2 1

SCORING

ABILITY TO DO

If you gave yourself scores of "1" or "2" on three or more items, first determine how important these items are to the type of consulting you plan to do. If they're not important, it may not affect your business at all. But if you have a low score on an item that seems to be essential, are you going to be able to acquire that ability?

WILLINGNESS TO DO

If you gave yourself scores of "1" or "2" on three or more items in this column, examine each problem area and determine how likely it will be required in your new life. If these things are required, then you need to carefully examine your level of commitment to your new business. If these are things you know must get done, and you aren't going to be willing to do them, then you must ask yourself if this type of consulting is really for you.

BE HONEST WITH YOURSELF

You may be able to fool all of the people some of the time and some of the people all of the time, but the one person you never can fool is yourself. Of course, you are eager to have your own business, but when you're making plans to go out on your own be sure you do it with your eyes wide open. It's your life and the only way to be sure of success is to be completely honest with yourself before you start down the road.

CHAPTER FIVE

Defining Your Business

Your future as a consultant will have a great deal to do with where you are offering your services. Geography is destiny in just about any business. You'd never expect to become a tycoon selling air conditioners in northern Maine or heating systems in Southern California. A family drugstore across the highway from a shopping mall is probably doomed to failure, as is a Hard Rock Café in a retirement village. As a consultant, you can plan to spread a wide net for clients and be prepared to move around a lot to serve them.

But before you make any decisions, make it your business to take a close look at the geographical area you've targeted. You might be surprised at what you'll find there—opportunities you hadn't noticed and competition you hadn't expected. Gather as much information as you can about the market, the competition, and, most important of all, about how you are going to fit into the mix. You can never do too much research when you're planning your new venture. You don't want to find yourself explaining in hindsight why it didn't work. And while you're gathering information, you may even find some pleasant surprises, but the only way to be sure that the surprises you'll find down the road are pleasant ones is to gather as much information as you possibly can *before* you start.

The first questions you should ask of yourself are, How many people in this area are doing what I want to do? Is the market glutted? Are there competitors with a lot of experience to offer, or are they coming into this business just because the idea interests them and they're willing to earn less while they learn it? How much do I want to earn, and how much are others being paid for the same kind of work?

Although not many consultants start their own businesses without having experience to back them up, it's surprising how many young people are skipping the step of working for someone else and going straight from college into business for themselves as consultants. Many have specialized degrees that make their knowledge valuable to companies that don't need or can't afford their expertise as full-time employees. Some leverage their lifestyles into niche markets such as fashion and retailing where staying ahead of the youth market is a matter of life and death. By and large, the living expenses of these people are lower and that means they can charge less.

Sometimes consultants can be in business for years before running into such competition, and the succesful ones make adjustments to the new reality. Making adjustments, in fact, is one of the first rules of consulting.

In most types of consultancy the client is paying for a new point of view, and when the situation changes, the client may change consultants too. Can you plan for such a thing? Probably not. But even when things don't go exactly according to plan, it's important to be able to react to change and turn it to your advantage. The reason why people hire consultants in the first place is for their expertise, but unless that expertise is a reflection of new trends and ideas, they are likely to go elsewhere in search of someone who is up to the minute. One way to solve a problem like that is to sign up the best of your new competitors as "associates." Chances are that they'll see it as an opportunity to learn from you. When you use them for specific asignments where a client is demanding tomorrow's answers to today's problems, the combination can make your service more valuable to clients who might otherwise have abandoned you.

LET YOUR NICHE EVOLVE

You need to make it a point to research the market before you go off on your own, but it is almost inevitable that you will eventually have to make adjustments as your business grows and the market changes. It is an experience many consultants face sooner or later. Although most create niches for themselves as experts in one area or another, one of the options all consultants share is the opportunity to open new doors when familiar ones are closed or become so familiar that the personal challenge is gone.

There is an endless variety of specialties in the consulting business, and niches within those specialties. If the niche you are determined to target turns out to be a crowded field, there is no reason to despair. The trick, of course, is to stand out in the crowd by doing it better. That is the best kind of niche you can find.

WRITE A BUSINESS PLAN

Many consultants have built successful practices advising entrepreneurs on small business start-ups, and the first step they often take is to write a business plan for their client. You may want to give a fellow consultant the job of writing yours, but doing it yourself could be a valuable experience.

The easiest way to get started is to take a short vacation. Alone. Take along a bunch of yellow pads, a few pens, and an open mind. Then, as you relax by a pool, on a beach, or next to a river or stream, take a hard look at where you want the future to take you. Go ahead and dream, but be honest with yourself. What you put on paper is going to help you follow your dream, and the last thing you need is to have your plan skewed by things you didn't really believe in the first place.

START WITH THE OBVIOUS

Some of the questions you should ask yourself may seem pretty obvious, like: What sort of business am I planning? and What services am I going to offer? But ask them anyway, and write down the answers. No detail is too insignificant.

You should consider why there is a need for this business of yours, where you are going to find your clients, and how much you can expect them to pay for your services. Sure, you may already have potential clients lined up, but you need to think about what you'll do if *their* business doesn't go according to plan before you've had a chance to help them.

You'll also need to make notes on the kind of office equipment and supplies you're going to need and what it all will probably cost. Be sure your business plan includes investments you've already made before you began dreaming this dream of yours. You may already have a computer, for instance, and it will be transformed from a toy into a business asset when you go out on your own.

If you're planning to work at home—and nearly all consultants begin that way—think about what it's going to cost to create a home office and an area for client meetings if your practice will require it. Even if you've already converted the front porch, write it down.

Your plan should also include what other consultants in your area have been up to, and what you're going to offer that's better. You'll also need to think about what kind of advertising and marketing it will take to let potential clients know what you can do for them.

Success is your goal, of course, and your business plan needs to spell out what you believe it's going to take to achieve it. And you need to touch all the bases, including how you'll be able to deal with unexpected setbacks. Naturally, you won't be able to predict every pothole down the road before you start, but you should have a battle plan to overcome them. Assess the trends in your industry over the past several years. It will put you in a better position to predict what might happen next and plan for the change.

THINK ABOUT THE MONEY

The most important thing you should consider is your financial plan, not just for this year but for at least five years into the future.

Your financial plan should begin with your start-up costs. Things like the installation of a business telephone line, insurance, accounting services, license fees, and association dues can add up fast, and none of them should come as a surprise. After you've added them up, project your operating costs, including supplies, utility bills, and taxes.

And whatever you do, don't forget your living expenses.

Now it's time to think about the money you expect to make. Break down the business you anticipate on a weekly and monthly basis and translate those estimates into an income statement. From there, you'll be able to determine what it's going to take to reach a break-even point. It will also help you predict profits and avoid any cash flow problems. Keep in mind that cash flow is what you're going to need to stay alive and ahead of the bill collectors. The profits will help make life worthwhile.

For most types of consultancy practices, it doesn't take a lot of

FINANCIAL READINESS

- What is the proper structure for your business? Should it be a sole proprietorship, a partnership, a limited liability company, or a corporation?
- How much money will it take to get your business started? What will you need to invest in equipment and supplies, setting up a workspace, promotional materials and fees?
- What type of insurance will you need? What will it cost?
- How much income do you need to support yourself (and your family) on a monthly basis?
- Where will you get the money? Have you explored all the alternatives with a financial expert?
- How long do you anticipate it will take for your business to become profitable?
- How will you support yourself (and your family) until it starts making a profit? How long can you support yourself this way?
- How much can your business afford in overhead? What will your normal overhead be?
- Do you understand: Bookkeeping principles? Cash flow? Balance sheets? Profit-and-loss statements? Sales forecasting?
- How well do you understand the market? Who is going to pay for your services?
- Who is your competition? What will you do if more competitors arrive on the scene?
- What will you charge for your services? What are your competitors charging?
- How will you deal with clients who don't pay on time? Or not at all?

cash to start, but unless you've figured out how to get along without money, or don't mind spending the rest of your life worrying about it, you are going to need to assess your financial picture before you make the decision to go off on your own.

TESTING YOUR FINANCIAL READINESS

The questionnaire on the previous page will help you gather the information you need before you get started. You may not have an immediate answer to all of the questions in the questionnaire, written by career guidance professional Charles L. Sodikoff, Ph.D. If you don't, ask your accountant or your friend at SCORE for help. Your financial analysis will be at the heart of your business plan.

DON'T LEAVE ANY STONES UNTURNED

Be specific and detailed in your answers. A plan based on dreams and not reality isn't worth the time it takes to write it out. Make sure your business plan isn't so rigid that it can't be changed after you've started your business or that it is too vague to be helpful. This is not just a document you'll write and file away, it is one of the most important working tools you can have. Your business plan should tell you, and anyone else who reads it, where you want to go—and, much more important, how you expect to get there.

CHAPTER SIX

Getting Started

At the heart of every consultant's practice is expertise for hire, and the basic tool of the trade is what Hercule Poirot calls "little gray cells." It isn't something you can go out and buy. You can enhance your brain power with education and there are courses you can take to hone your skills or learn new ones. But apart from talent, training, and experience, just what does it take to get started as a consultant? Not much in the way of tools or equipment, it turns out. In the end, as George Harrison of the Beatles was fond of pointing out, "It's all in the mind, you know."

That said, in this age of technology there are some investments that you may need to make as you're getting started, but they may not be as expensive as you think. Public relations consultant Jim McClure, whose clients are mostly large telecommunications corporations, says, "I have better equipment right here in my house than most of the people I work with have in their offices," but if you were to take a tour of Jim's home office you might wonder what he's talking about. His computer isn't brand-new, his modem isn't super-fast, his laser printer isn't state-of-the-art. He doesn't have a high-speed copying machine, he makes do with two telephone lines, and he doesn't have a fancy voice-mail system, just an old-fashioned answering machine. He does have a cellular telephone, though, because, as he puts it, "I have to stay reachable. When a client calls, it's too easy for them to call someone else if I'm not at my desk."

Then what is it that makes him feel better equipped than those high-powered executives who pride themselves on being technologically up-to-the-minute? "When you're dealing with corporate clients," he explains, "almost none of them has direct access to the Internet. Very few of them even have modems. They are hooked up through corporate LANs—local area networks—and all they have is access to internal E-mail. It's just about impossible for an outside contractor to get through the firewalls of those corporate systems. And none of them will work with anybody who can't hand-deliver proposals, presentations, and reports. Yes, of course you can't run a business these days without faxes, E-mail, and the Internet, but you'll find some clients who still require you to handle business the old-fashioned way with personal contact."

The fact is, though, such clients are rare, and a consultant who isn't computer literate is on the road to failure. Your consultancy business is going to revolve around proposals, presentations, and reports. And thanks to computers they're easier to produce than ever before, but ease is just part of the story. Clients in every field are demanding electronic literacy in everyone they work with, and that, obviously, means you are going to need a computer. You probably already have one, but since you're planning to restart your life with a clean slate, you might want to find out what's different out there since the last time you looked. Your computer is going to become as important to your new life as a car in suburbia, and you're going to need it to be trouble-free.

TAKE A SHOPPING TRIP

Even if you don't think you're going to need to buy one, computer shopping is something like going to a boat show. And every bit as much fun. Nearly everything you see will tempt you, but it's also pretty simple to talk yourself out of buying everything you see. When all is said and done, most consultants, except those in the computer field, don't really need much in the way of computer equipment. But you're going to be surprised at what is available.

A SIMPLE SHOPPING LIST

In general, a computer's role in a consulting practice is handling word processing, sending and receiving E-mail, keeping a calendar and a to-do list, and browsing the Internet. None of these things demand high technology or high speed, except possibly in a modem. And that means unless you're going to play three-dimensional games, handle graphics programs, or complicated financial analysis programs, you can probably do very well with a low-cost PC. Try it before you buy it, but, for the most part, the new crop of desktop computers selling for under a thousand dollars are just as reliable as higher-priced ones. Look for a computer that has at least 32 megabytes of RAM (random access memory) and a 4-gigabyte hard drive. It should have a 15-inch monitor, a 24-speed CD ROM, and 56K V90 modem. Yes, all of this is standard in most low-cost computers these days, and it may well be all you're going to need.

One thing that may surprise you if you haven't explored this world in a while is the prices. Computers still aren't cheap, but most companies are offering good values for under a thousand dollars these days, and even those prices are dropping fast while the list of features goes up, almost on a daily basis.

When you go computer shopping you'll find that prices vary from catalog to catalog and from store to store (you may even find that the price on the shelf is negotiable). It's a good idea to shop around, but bargains aren't the only thing you should be looking for. A computer that's short on memory or isn't compatible with the software you need now or in the future isn't worth the space it takes up on your desk.

You are going to meet some computer salespeople who will remind you of used-car salesmen, which may be why the industry term for them is "resellers." Of course, you can expect them to know a lot about their products and you can learn a lot by listening to them, but don't let them talk you into buying things you don't need or can't use. Do your homework first. Talk with people who use computers as well as the ones who sell them. Take a trip on the Internet and visit computer-related websites. Read computer magazines and newspapers and send away for information from their advertisers. The exercise can help make you an expert on computer buying and, who knows, you might make that a part of your consultancy. Think of all the people who can use the advice.

YOU CAN TAKE IT WITH YOU

As a consultant, you'll probably be working away from your own office a great deal of the time, and it may make sense to be able to take your office with you in the form of a laptop computer.

These machines, which were once to desktop computers what portable typewriters were to IBM Selectrics, have been dramatically improved in recent years and there isn't much you won't be able to accomplish with one. Most inexpensive laptops weigh seven or eight pounds, many newer models are even lighter, but batteries and additional add-on drives will add to their heft, as will AC power supplies. The current generation of laptops generally has all the power and features you need already built in, but if you find you are going to want to add to it, be careful to buy products that are compatible.

You can do very well with a fifteen-hundred-dollar investment in a machine that comes with a 4-gigabyte hard drive, a CD-

ROM player, and a modem, but prices for a much speedier laptop can run up to six thousand. On the other hand, as with everything else in the computer business, prices are dropping.

For speed, common wisdom has it that your laptop needs to have an Intel-based system. In fact, a rumor around Silicon Valley a few years ago was that when Apple founder Steve Jobs bought a laptop for his college-bound daughter, it was an IBM ThinkPad. But whether that's true or not, Macintosh has been steadily catching up since then and its newer PowerBooks are actually faster than the competition. Then again, there are other features to consider besides speed, so even if you believe a laptop computer will make your life easier, don't buy the first one you see.

If you haven't checked out laptops lately, among the improvements you are going to see are batteries that last longer than they used to, but no matter how sophisticated the technology has become, they are still batteries and are prone to run out of juice at the worst possible time. When that happens, the computer slows down and then stops, no matter what kind of chip is inside. This can take all the joy out of being able to work under a beach umbrella. A way to limit the problem, if not avoid it altogether, is to buy lithium replacement batteries. They cost more, something like two hundred twenty-five dollars compared to one hundred seventy-five dollars for NiMH (nickel and metal hydride) technology, but they last longer. Many of the new laptops come with lithium batteries as original equipment.

The laptop's battery gauge is designed to tell you how much power you have available, but it may not be as reliable as you've been led to believe. When in doubt, plug it in. And when you leave home, take along a spare battery and consider investing in an external battery recharger. And, remember, the battery drains even when you have the laptop's power turned off, so when you're not using it, keep it plugged in!

About once a month or so, you should "burp" your battery.

That is, let it run dry and then recharge it fully. Leave the AC adapter turned on and take the battery out for about thirty seconds. Then replace it and recharge it. The average laptop battery is good for about five hundred rechargings.

Although laptop computers are more fragile than desktop models, they are, of course, very similar. There are, however, some differences you should consider. Lower-cost models are equipped with "passive-matrix" screens, sometimes called "dual-scan," which require a little adjusting the first time you turn them on. In some cases, illumination on these screens is uneven and there can be shadow images to contend with. This may make it difficult for you to keep track of the cursor.

Passive-matrix laptop screens also have a narrow viewing angle, which means that if you're not looking straight at the screen, you're going to see a murky image at best. If you spend a lot of time working with any kind of laptop, make it a point to take frequent breaks. The limited viewing angle forces you to sit in one position for too long and you may begin to feel a nagging pain between your shoulders. The narrow viewing angle can also be a problem if a client is looking over your shoulder to see what you're doing.

You don't have to be worried about the health effects of spending a lot of time too close to a laptop computer screen, though. These thin, flat screens use a technology called LCD (liquid crystal display), the same as your digital watch. There are no electrical emmissions from them and no danger of radiation. Illumination is lower than with desktop screens, though, so if you spend long hours staring at a laptop screen, eyestrain could be a problem. Some desktops are already available with LCD screens, which save a huge amount of desk space. Needless to say, they are quite expensive. But count on it, prices will drop and one of these days it's a sure bet that LCD will be the standard for all computer screens.

"Active-matrix" screens are more expensive because they are

produced abroad and are subject to higher import duties than most other electronic equipment. However, they come equipped with brightness and contrast controls and the picture is much sharper. Better still, you can see it from the side, which is good news for your aching back. But in spite of the advantages, you may not find the added cost worthwhile.

If you are considering using a laptop computer exclusively, keep in mind that the screen is smaller and that means you're going to have to do more scrolling to keep track of your work. The keyboard is smaller, too, and for some harder to manipulate than a desktop system.

No matter how convenient a portable computer may be, many people who use them also have desktop models and transfer files from laptop to desktop. There are several ways this is accomplished, including moving files back and forth on a floppy disk, but among the easiest of them for average users is to have a permanent docking station. If you are going on a trip, you don't need to carry extra drives you won't need, and when you get back to the office you simply attach the laptop to its dock where such things as a big color monitor and full keyboard allow you to use your laptop as a regular desktop without investing in two machines. However, the newer generations of laptops are as fully equipped as many desktops in terms of memory and other features, so unless you're interested in keyboard comfort and the convenience of a bigger color monitor, you probably won't want to spend the extra money on a docking station.

WHAT SHOULD IT BE: MAC OR PC?

In the computer world, there is one question that will never get you a simple answer: Should you buy an Apple Macintosh or IBM-compatible system?

The people who prefer one over the other are like religious fanatics and they'll do everything they can to convert you to their way of thinking, but when all is said and done, the choice you'll make is a very personal one, and it may depend on your past experience with computers. However, if you are going to be interfacing with your clients' computers, it is imperative that your system and its software be compatible with the platforms they are using.

There was once a time when an IBM machine would clam up like a kid faced with a plate of spinach when it was fed a disk created on an Apple computer, and the reverse was also true. Newer machines have eliminated the problem, but it still takes a bit of coaxing before one will recognize the competition, and it is best to be able to give your clients files they can use without too much bother.

In general, most corporations and other large businesses are IBM-equipped; book publishers, ad agencies, and others that use extensive graphics are more likely to be using Macs. Of course, since the introduction of Microsoft Windows, the graphics capabilities of the IBM PC and its clones have become more like Macs, if not still harder to learn. Any IBM fan will be quick to tell you that there is more software available for their preferred platform. But Mac people will respond that they are referring to video games and such things that have nothing to do with your business. On the other hand, if you use the newest versions of Microsoft Word, the most popular word processing program, you'll probably find that it is more IBM-friendly.

When all is said and done, make it a point to find out which platform is the standard in your particular industry—not only will it add to your professional image, but it will save time both for you and your clients.

WHAT MORE DO YOU NEED?

The average consultant doesn't need much more than a reliable computer with faxing capability and Internet access. But you'll need a thing or two to keep that computer reliable and avoid problems you don't need.

It's a rare computer user who hasn't at one time or another kept right on working through a thunderstorm. Their machines were plugged into a surge protector and there didn't seem to be any reason to shut down. Then came that flash of lightning, a blank screen, and a morning's work lost forever.

Naturally, their computer-savvy friends didn't have much sympathy for them. "You have to save your work constantly," they clucked, "and back up your work at the end of every day." Yes, of course. You should brush your teeth after every meal, too. But sometimes you forget, and most of the time it doesn't seem to make a lot of difference.

When your computer loses electrical power, it forgets what it was doing and chances are when you get it up and running again you have to rely on your own memory to pick up the thread. How often you save your files depends on how much time you want to spend recovering lost ideas. It's a matter of choosing one keystroke over hundreds.

Regardless of how often you save your files, never plug your computer into anything but a surge protector, or even better an uninterrupted power supply (UPS). For as little as a hundred dollars, a UPS will provide protection for your whole system from the computer itself to your modem, your printer, your fax machine, and your storage drives. Not only that, but it supresses surges in telephone lines while you're online. Many models will also automatically save data and shut down the computer when the power fails.

Putting each day's work on a separate disk makes sense, too. But it's one more thing to remember, and if you are like most people, you probably won't bother—especially if you are in the middle of a detailed report and plan to pick up where you left off tomorrow morning. But no matter what else you do, you should make it a point to save each job—every letter, every presentation, every report—on a disk. Consider it your file copy. When a project is finished, you can remove it from your hard disk and free up some space there. In fact, having all of a particular client's work on floppy disks will make it much easier to find than searching through everything on your hard drive.

Computer salesmen may try to talk you into big storage systems like zip or cartridge drives like jaz, but unless you are putting together an encyclopedia or need to store photographs or artwork, you probably don't need them. You may find one useful for file storage or backing up your system, but if you are just producing average-size documents, a box of high-density floppy disks will serve you very well for a fraction of the price.

Most computers come equipped with CD-ROM drives these days (shorthand for "compact disk read-only memory"). You are going to need one because a lot of software and reference material you'll be using is delivered only on CD-ROMs.

A computer is useless without a monitor, but you don't need anything fancy. Chances are you don't even need it to display color images, but you'd probably have to scour junkyards to find a black-and-white one. Something you should consider, though, is that a larger screen might be worthwhile in cutting down your scrolling time. The 15-inch monitors that come with most computer packages don't display a full page of text at one time, and you'll find yourself scrolling back and forth to see what you've been saying. Beyond that, when you shop for a monitor, the best thing to do is simply look at the screen and see for yourself what you're going to be looking at for a long time to come. Eyestrain shouldn't be an occupational disease you'll have to deal with.

Nor should carpal tunnel syndrome, a painful wrist-nerve disorder that strikes many computer users. The keyboard you select—and there are dozens to choose from—will help you avoid it, so road-test a few for comfort before you buy one. It is also well worth investing in a hand rest or a keyboard that has one built into it. A twist of the wrist can put you out of business.

Computer makers consider printers an optional extra even though you can't function without one. They can reproduce in black-and-white or color and they come in three basic types: dot-matrix, inkjet, and laser. The output of dot-matrix printers tends to be ragged, and are not recommended as a way to put your best face forward; besides, the cost of better-quality inkjet printers keeps dropping and their noisy, slow dot-matrix cousins are quickly becoming museum pieces. You still see them in computer stores and catalogs because they are excellent for printing multiple-copy forms as well as checks, receipts, and other business documents. A dot-matrix printer is a lot like an old-fashioned typewriter, right down to the ribbon.

A laser printer works like a Xerox machine, using a laser diode to transfer an image to a cylindrical drum that uses an electrostatic process to attract toner particles (the powder that creates the printed image) and fuse them to a page with heated rollers. Some are better than others, but it takes a laser printer to deliver the best quality possible. That doesn't mean you need one, though, unless your computer printouts are going to be used as art for a commercial printer.

For most applications in your consulting business, you'll get along very well with an inkjet printer to create the clean hard copy you need, and chances are you don't have to go to the expense of buying one that prints in color. There are may variations on the inkjet theme as newer technology brings them closer to laser-quality. Among the leaders in this quest for more color and realism is the Canon Corporation, whose Bubble jet printers print color photographs almost as close to the original as the output of more expensive laser printers.

If you get an inkjet printer, make sure you have a spare ink supply in your desk. These printers spray ink onto the page from a sealed cartridge, but very few will warn you when they're running dry—they just spew out blank pages as though nothing has happened.

Just as important as print quality is printing speed. Keep it in mind when you're looking at printers because, while most computers have a "background printing" feature that allows you to get on with your work while a document is being printed, there will be times when you you want that printed copy right now, and you'll be grateful for a speedy response.

If you work with photographs, a new breed of flatbed scanner not only gets the images into your computer but also doubles as a laser printer, copier, and a fax machine, too. When you're shopping for one, remember that a copier and a printer aren't the same thing. All scanners function as copiers, but only the more expensive ones also incorporate a printer. You can also use them to scan text into your computer. A budget version of this multitalented machine is priced well below three hundred dollars, but even the best of them come in at around one thousand.

GET CONNECTED

Among the basic tools for most consultancy practices is Internet access and E-mail capability. For that, you're going to need a modem (an abbreviation of the technical term, modulator-demodulator) to get connected. Most modems also receive and send faxes through telephone lines at 9,600 or 14,400 bits per second, which is known as the baud rate. The current standard modem speed, which is changing like everything else in this field, is 33.6 Bps (bits per second). High numbers mean that your modem will be capable of compressing the data it sends so it will take less time. A higher baud rate will allow you to cruise the Internet and download information at higher speeds, too, although there are variables, such as the efficiency of the online service you are using and the limitations of your telephone line. For faxing, however, your modem can only be as fast as the one at the other end of the line.

You should also have a separate phone line for for your modem. When your telephone is connected to your computer, you can't receive calls.

In some areas, telephone companies are offering ISDN (integrated services digital network) lines which combine voice and digital transmission on a single line. It costs more, but if you are planning to download large files on a regular basis or find that browsing the Web takes more patience than you can muster, it may be worth the extra cost. On the horizon, and available now in some places, is ADSL (asymmetrical digital subscriber lines), which allows you to move data as much as two hundred and fifty times faster than on an ordinary phone line. It is expensive, too. Like ISDN, the service requires special modems, higher installation fees, and much higher monthly service fees—an old-fashioned analog phone line costs, on average, about twenty dollars per month, while ISDN service rarely costs less than one hundred per month for service alone. ADSL service, if it is available in your area, typically costs a bit less on a monthly basis thanks to introductory promotions, but installation can be as much as six hundred dollars. A big advantage, though, is that ADSL lines aren't metered and you'll get unlimited service for your monthly fee.

If you plan to use your modem to send and receive faxes, keep in mind that most of them won't receive one if your computer isn't turned on. So if you expect to get faxes in the middle of the night or on your day off, it's a good idea to put a standard desktop fax machine on your shopping list as well. Invest in a plain-paper fax so you can use it like a copying machine to reproduce letters and other documents.

A copying machine may be an expense you can avoid. There are more places to have copies made in most neighborhoods than there are barbershops. And if you are making copies of multipage documents, it's cheaper to let the copy shop handle them than to eat into your own time.

GET ONLINE

A great deal of the work any consultant does involves research. Until not very long ago, that meant spending time in libraries leafing through books and files. Just getting to and from the source of information was time-consuming, and the research time revolved around the library's hours. That has become a thing of the past thanks to the World Wide Web. Not only can you download more information than even the biggest libraries can provide, but the Web is never closed. You can find what you need to know in the wee hours of the morning, you can check facts before that 9 A.M. meeting, and you can find answers before the client has forgotten the question.

But research is only one reason why you need online access. Being able to send and receive E-mail between your office and your clients' helps save an incredible amount or time. You can send a detailed report in less time (and at less cost) than it takes to fill out the form to send it overnight.

And there is another reason, too. One of the most difficult transitions people experience when they shift from working in an office to working at home alone is not having interaction with other people for help and encouragement. As a consultant, you will be in the people business, but you may have less personal interaction than when you had coworkers. Many consultants have found a way around that by chatting online with others who can help bring problem-solving into focus.

For doing research on the Web, you probably need a good Internet server that will help you skirt around the web. Services like America Online, MSN, or Compuserve, will give you Web access, too, and their chatrooms and newsgroups will help you get in on the fun of keeping in touch.

COMPUTER SOFTWARE

It's against the rules to rent, borrow, or steal computer software, but even if it weren't forbidden to copy someone else's programs, it isn't a good idea. The technical support that software developers provide to registered owners through 800 numbers and the manuals you get when you buy their programs are worth their weight in gold. When you've promised to deliver a report first thing in the morning and a software glitch pops up unexpectedly, you're going to be grateful for the help, but don't forget to fill out the registration forms that come with the software and keep the registration numbers handy—they're your passwords to the help lines.

The kind of software you're going to need depends on your speciality. For example, as an urban planner, Barbara Arnold uses CAD (computer-assisted drafting) programs regularly, but for most types of consultancies a reliable word processing program may be all that is necessary.

There are several word processing programs to choose from, but far and away the most popular is Microsoft Word. The instruction book that comes with it is close to nine hundred pages long, and you can take an endless number of courses to delve into all its intricacies, but by and large, once it's installed on your hard drive, using it is as simple as typing. There are simpler programs that can do the job, of course, but you'll get better results from Word or another super word-cruncher, such as WordPerfect. And more likely than not you'll be compatible with your clients.

Once you get comfortable with one of these programs, you'll find that there isn't much you won't be able to do. If your consultancy involves creating brochures or annual reports or other things desktop publishers have made their speciality, you'll want to add graphics programs to your bag of tricks. In general, though, unless you have a lot of time, a lot of patience, and a lot of RAM, you're probably better off leaving those to your neighborhood desktop publisher.

It is a rare consultant who doesn't rank a cellular telephone as the most important tool they have. They have become so much a part of our lives it is hard to believe that the first cell phone call was made only as recently as 1983.

If you are not among the fifty million people who already have a cellular telephone, you are going to find so many different options available it may boggle your mind. There is stiff competition among companies that provide the service, and about 15 percent of all users switch carriers every year to take advantage of better deals. The number might be higher if the majority weren't locked into long-term service contracts with stiff cancellation fees.

Before you sign one of those contracts, go over the fine print with a fine-tooth comb. Things are not always what they seem. Most carriers require a minimum monthly fee, which you'll pay whether you use the phone or not. To make the cost seem lower, most companies offer "free" calling time, usually on weekends. You will also have to pay for "airtime" every minute you are on the phone and that includes calls you receive as well as the ones you make.

Although analog cellular telephones go for anywhere from one hundred fifty to three hundred dollars, it is possible to get one for just a few dollars or even free if you sign a one-year service contract. But "free" is a tricky word. *Consumer Reports* says that a carrier typically earns more than five hundred dollars a year from subscribers who paid next to nothing for the hardware.

Many cell phone contracts also offer such free amenities as conferencing, call-forwarding, paging, and voice mail, all of which are useful to a consultant. However, the free offer isn't forever and eventually you'll be expected to pay extra for them.

Although not available everywhere yet, digital PCS (personal communications service) phones are clearly the wave of the future. With the now–old-fashioned analog phones, calls are often arbitrarily dropped or disconnected, and if you are using one in your car, you can experience ragged transmission as you move around. Worse, it is relatively easy for eavesdroppers to monitor your conversations and even clone your phone, leaving you stuck with their long-distance charges. PCS phones use an encoding process that makes such things nearly impossible. They also make dropped and disconnected calls a thing of the past. Better still, because they are close cousins to your computer, you can easily use a digital cell phone to download faxes and receive and send E-mail by connecting to your computer.

Possibly the biggest advantage of a PCS phone is that batteries last longer than with analog phones. You can leave it on standby to receive calls for almost two days without replacing the battery pack and actually use the phone for four full hours. Try that with an analog cell phone and the batteries will be dead in half the time.

It is only a matter of time before PCS phones become the standard, and stiff competition among carriers guarantees that costs will drop. Still, though the costs may appear to be high, they aren't prohibitive even now. In the New York area, where a new customer can get an analog telephone for less than ten dollars with a contract, a digital model costs about one hundred seventy-five dollars, and the pricing plan under the contract that comes with it is more generous.

PCS service isn't available everywhere quite yet, and if you travel a lot, consider buying a cellular phone that combines both digital and analog capabilities. It will automatically switch from one to the other depending on availability.

In some types of consultancy, as an interior decorator for instance, it may make sense to rent space in a downtown area convenient for your clients. Others, like management consultants or public relations experts who work in urban settings, may find it to their advantage to rent desk space in an office building at a convenient or prestigious address. In most cases, the rental includes the use of a conference room as well as a telephone answering service.

Most computer consultants can't do their work anywhere except at their clients' offices. But while many consultants in other fields find it necessary to do some work on-site, most rarely prefer it as a steady diet. When MaryAnn Friedlander went off on her own her first client demanded her presence on-site, but she says that "clients think they own you when you work there every day." As soon as the project was finished, she set up her own home office and now doesn't often accept assignments that can't be done there.

Where you do your work as a consultant obviously depends on the kind of consultancy you are establishing. Sometimes a downtown office may be necessary for your clients' convenience or to enhance your professional image, but with few exceptions, there is no reason why you shouldn't be planning to set up an office in your home. Vickie Sherman, for one, says "I plan to keep working from the office I had built in my home for as long as I possibly can. Among other things, there are excellent tax advantages."

Some types of consultancy require meetings in your office, but that, apparently, is a problem most who work out of their homes don't consider a roadblock. Barbara Arnold, whose specialty is urban planning, converted the dining room in her Buffalo, New York, home into an office, but says that "I also have a war room upstairs that doubles as a conference room." MaryAnn Friedlander makes it a point to schedule meetings at clients' offices, but when that isn't possible she says she uses the local coffee shop. And Michael Nelson, who specializes in management consulting, more often than not meets with clients in their offices. But he routinely meets them at the local Kinko's. "They are much better-equipped with telecommunications gear than I am," he says, "and that is an asset. You'd be surprised at the people you can meet there, too. That place is the 90's answer to the old town pump." Coffee shops also work well for casual meetings, but for a more professional setting, some consultants rent meeting rooms in hotels or establish a relationship with restaurants that have private rooms. Still others find membership in a club worthwhile for making an impression on clients. But you may find that there is no place like home for some client meetings.

Patricia Bruneau, a Northern California wedding consultant, meets with her clients in her living room. "It makes them feel more comfortable," she says. Working at home can make you feel more comfortable, too, and may make you more efficient. Most types of consultancy don't take up a lot of space and a home office cuts down on your overhead. Even though not everyone finds that living and working in the same place is the best way to run a business, most independent consultants seem to find it an amicable match. For one thing, it gives them uninterrupted time to get their work done, and you certainly can't beat the rent.

However, when you put together an office in your home, be very careful not to confuse your two lives. Your workspace may be under the same roof as your bed-and-breakfast nook, but you're going to need to think of it as a completely different world. That's what the IRS expects you to do, and even if you've got files and books and papers strewn all over the house, it isn't going to cut it with them. It shouldn't with you, either. You will be working for a living, but don't make the mistake of living with your work.

To paraphrase the sign over the salad bar, take all the space you need, but use all the space you take. And not a square foot more. Don't let your work spill over into your living space. Those magazines and books and computer printouts belong near your desk and not on the coffee table in the living room. Be obsessive about it. Your business will infiltrate your personal life if you're not. And you know what they say about all work and no play. It makes for a dull life.

It is important to have a separate telephone line for your business, too. (No, not the one connected to your modem, a *different* one.) That way, you'll always be sure it will be answered in a professional way and besides, it's easier. The IRS requires you to keep business and personal calls separate in your tax records.

Keep your business phone lines in the part of the house where you'll be doing business because that's where your records and logs ought to be. Apart from having the kids answer your business telephone, one of the most unprofessional things you can do is to ask a client to hold the phone while you run from the kitchen to your office to look something up.

It goes without saying that when clients call you should be able to put your finger on their files without a long search. That means you need to keep your workspace organized. You might think that since the office is your private domain, neatness doesn't count. You may even have a sign there that says "a sloppy desk is a sign of a creative mind," but don't believe a word of it. Let your creativity show in problem solving, not on your desk.

That isn't to say that your office should always look like you're expecting a photographer from a home decorating magazine to drop by. However, suppose a client calls out of the blue to talk about a contract? Your mind is lost in the job you're working on and you can't for the life of you put your hands on that piece of paper. But for the life of your business, you'd better be able to. If your office isn't organized, you won't be, either. And if you're not organized, you're not only going to waste a lot of time, but you're going to miss opportunities, too.

CAN YOU GO IT ALONE?

Most consultants make it a point to stay in touch with other experts in their field and call on them for help when they need it. Consultants depend on constant networking and their Rolodexes are among their most important tools. As a consultant, however, for the most part you're going to be like a one-man band, doing everything from drumming up business to taking the applause for a job well done. By definition, that is the price you'll pay for your independence.

You are going to have just one product to sell: yourself. You will be marketing your experience, your talent, and your personal approach to problem solving. Does that mean you're not going to need any outside help beyond your own area of expertise? Not exactly.

WILL YOU NEED A LAWYER?

You probably won't need to keep an attorney at your beck and call, but it's a good idea to talk to one at the start to make sure you don't get off on the wrong foot. For one thing, you'll need to give serious thought to the form your business should take. As one lawyer explains it, "If your business fails, you can lose your house, your car, and everything you own unless you take the right steps before you start. And that includes setting up some form of corporation to protect yourself."

Deciding which form your business should take is only one of the reasons why you'll need legal help. There will be legal papers to file at the start, too. And for some types of consultancy, such as those involving health care, financial planning, or engineering, licenses to apply for as well. Most important of all, every assignment you take on should begin with a written contract, and you will need professional advice to draft a form that makes sure all the bases are covered, including ways to avoid collection problems. Obviously, you won't need to check with a lawyer every time you draft a contract, but it's a good idea to have one help you develop some guidelines at the beginning.

Since your business is essentially advice for a price, the possibility always exists that your advice might be construed as a reason for ultimate failure. That's why it is a very good idea to follow up on every assignment even after you've signed off on it. When things go wrong, a client may not call you to find out why, but might be more likely to pick up the phone and call a lawyer. Your best insurance against such a thing is to have access to a lawyer who understands your specialty. You want to avoid lawsuits at all costs.

The best place to look for a lawyer who will understand your business is by calling the local bar association. In most places, they'll provide you with a list of attorneys in the area whose experience best suits your needs and they'll give you some idea of how much you can expect to be charged. Many of these lawyers will also give you a short consultation at no charge, which will give you an opportunity to sample the synergy before you pay a retainer. You can also ask other consultants or people who are running other small businesses for recommendations. The experts at SCORE can be helpful here, too, especially if you're on a limited budget.

Legal fees vary from place to place and from lawyer to lawyer, and everything else being equal, it will pay to do a little comparison shopping. You may find that you'll only have to pay a small fee for the paperwork you need to get started because much of that kind of work is done by paralegals in a law firm's office, but for a consultation, you're going to be paying by the hour.

With that in mind, you ought to have some idea what your options are before you sit down in a lawyer's office. To make sure you'll be able to touch all the bases in short order, go there with a written list of questions.

WHAT FORM SHOULD YOUR BUSINESS TAKE?

Many consultants operate as though they were still on someone else's payroll. Their businesses are usually called "sole proprietorships," but accountants often refer to them as Schedule C businesses for the federal income tax forms they are required to file. But the problem with a proprietorship is that your personal assets and your business assets get all mixed up. Not only that, but your spouse's assets are mixed in there, too, which may be taking more of a chance on love than you bargained for.

As far as the tax people are concerned, as a sole proprietor, your income from your business is no different than if you were earning a salary. It's the same with your creditors. Your business debts are the same to them as your personal ones, and if your business gets into trouble (yes, it can happen), you might find your personal bank accounts frozen. You need to have a way to separate business from pleasure or you can lose everything you own whether it has anything to do with your business or not.

A legal partnership, like a sole proprietorship, also makes no distinction between your personal and your business assets. And to make matters worse, you don't have the same amount of control over either one because you have your partner's input to contend with.

As a consultant, you are marketing your own expertise, and a partnership may not be among your options. There may be exceptions, however. For instance, if you are involved in a consultancy that calls for expertise in different areas, a partnership might make sense. You may have a dream partner in mind, but remember that dreams are close cousins of nightmares. If your partner dips too deeply into the company's profits, for a family emergency for instance, you are going to have to make up the difference. If your partner decides to walk away and your company has any debts, you will be required to make good on them yourself. That could take away all your savings, your house, your car, and everything you or your spouse owns. Yes, it's a worst-case scenario—but it does happen.

The moral is, Be very careful when you go into a partnership with anybody. If you find over time that your partnership isn't a marriage made in heaven—and it happens all the time—dissolving it can be as messy as any divorce.

Chances are you aren't thinking of forming a partnership anyway, and even though you may be thinking big, forming a corporation is probably out of the question, too. In the world of big business, investors form corporations and declare themselves shareholders as a kind of ultimate protection from personal risk. If the corporation goes bankrupt, they are not responsible for anything other than their original investment. But before you consider issuing stock in your new venture, you need to consider the downside. It's a big one.

You'll owe the federal government a huge tax on any profits you make, and many states also levy their own corporate tax on top of that. If you pay yourself any dividends, you'll have to report them on your personal income tax return, and that means you'll be paying tax on money that has already been taxed.

Still, when you become an independent consultant you are forming a business whether you think of it that way or not and you are going to need the protection that comes with formalizing it. And it may be simpler than you imagined.

For small businesses like yours, the IRS has come up with a different kind of structure it calls Subchapter S. It gives you all the benefits of being incorporated without most of the burdens. Basically, Subchapter S allows business and professional people to be considered a corporation except when the time comes to pay the taxes. Subchapter S companies don't pay corporate income taxes on their profits. Instead, their owners are taxed just once, on April 15. They are allowed to deduct business losses and expenses, which can reduce their personal income taxes, especially at the beginning when they are reinvesting their profits in the business. There are some restrictions to the Subchapter S scenario, but not many of them will affect your consulting business.

There are even fewer limitations with a new kind of business form that has come on the scene, a limited liability company, which offers more of the kinds of protection that investors in large corporations enjoy, but is taxed like a partnership or a sole proprietorship. Like a partnership, they have a predetermined life, usually thirty years, which can be extended. And in some states, though not all, they need to have the earmarks of a partnership with a requirement that at least two persons form the company.

A limited liability company might be the best way for you to go. The revised federal tax law of 1996 made Subchapter S companies more like LLCs, but there are still differences. Those that will affect you when you are starting up your new business are more likely to be on the local level. Some states don't recognize the Subchapter S concept, for instance, and they tax such companies as unincorporated businesses.

Because there are so many variables, you *absolutely* must talk to your lawyer or your accountant about them before you make a decision. Not only will it save you money every tax year, but it will protect your personal assets as well.

WILL YOU NEED AN ACCOUNTANT?

Many consultancies involve financial planning and some, like management consulting, require a background in financial matters. But being savvy about money isn't a requirement for all types of consultancy practices. Does that mean the services of an accountant is required?

Very few consultants say they use an accountant for anything more than handling their tax returns. Some find it handy to be able to check in with one every couple of months to make sure that their actual income is squaring with the estimate they made last April. If it isn't, an accountant can help them decide if it is worthwhile to adjust their quarterly estimated payments to the IRS and avoid an unexpected bill next April. The same road check, by the way, can also reduce your quarterly payments if you're not making money as fast as you thought you would.

Some independent consultants use financial software on their computers to do the work of an accountant, but most say they prefer going to a professional when they can. Although income from consulting doesn't usually involve collecting and paying sales tax, the rules do vary from city to city. An accountant can spare you the problems of dealing with local taxes if you live in an area where they are considered your responsibility.

Irwin Fenichel, a partner in the New York City accounting firm of Edward Isaacs & Company LLP, says that most small business people such as consultants use his firm's services for taxes, financial statements, and bookkeeping. In his experience, most entrepreneurial types "have a careless attitude about money." (Sound like anybody *you* know?) He says that he finds most of them have more faith in the future than they probably should and don't usually care about going into debt to get themselves over the rough spots because they have faith that they are going to hit it big one of these days. That may be a great outlook on life but, as he puts it, "they need an accountant to rein them in a little."

When he works with a new small business start-up, his key consideration is capital and financing. In just about every small business, including consulting where not much investment is required, there can be long months at the beginning when there is no money coming in to take care of daily expenses. He wants to be sure a new businessperson will be able to deal with it because there is usually nowhere for them to turn for help. "Banks aren't very comfortable with new businesses," he warns, "and even less so with service businesses like consulting."

When Fenichel studies a client's financial statements, he looks carefully at business plans with special attention on projections. "Banks do, too," he points out. But the most important thing he looks for is debt-to-equity because "a heavily leveraged business has a serious problem." You may be deeper in debt than you realize, by the way. Many small business people admit to having maxed out their credit cards to get started, and usually say they don't consider it a debt like a bank loan because they've been making credit card payments for as long as they can remember. But a bank loan is exactly what it is. The most expensive kind there is, in fact.

On the subject of bank loans, Fenichel also warns that banks generally require a personal guarantee before considering them, especially for first-time borrowers. This means that if you're thinking of applying for a loan at a bank, you may be required to provide such collateral as your home or personal and business assets to guarantee it. Because the value of your computer and most of your office equipment is dropping so rapidly, it isn't usually accepted as collateral.

As for hiring an accountant, Irwin Fenichel advises that, "It's a two-way street. Both parties need to be comfortable with one another and I need to feel confident that I can recommend clients to a bank when they need help."

MONEY MATTERS

Without an accountant, you may have a hard time keeping up with all the information that is crucial to your business—items such as overhead and accounts receivable. Your accountant will be able to help you determine how much cash flow you need to stay afloat and blow the whistle when money isn't coming in fast enough. If you find you need a loan or a line of credit to keep you going, your accountant will put together the paperwork a lender wants to see and then not only give you advice about what sort of loan you should ask for and what protection you'll need but will recommend the best place to take your application.

Your lawyer can probably recommend an accountant who can serve your specific needs. Or you might also ask other small business people in your neighborhood to share their experiences in finding help to keep up with the financial side of their businesses.

ARE YOU INSURED FOR THAT?

Either your lawyer or your accountant can be helpful in recommending the kinds of insurance you need to have. Some liability insurance plans are available with riders that can protect you in lawsuits, for instance. You'll need protection against fire and theft, too, and if you invite clients to meetings in your home office, you'll need added liability coverage. Most important of all, though, you'll certainly need a medical insurance policy, preferably one that will help keep your business functioning—and your family fed—if you need to be hospitalized. In addition to losing a steady paycheck when you strike out on your own, you are also losing all those fringe benefits that come with a steady job. Remember, there is so such thing as a sick day when you're in business for yourself.

Many independent consultants have medical insurance through their working spouses. They're the lucky ones. What if you're single or supporting a family on your own? Health insurance rates for individuals can sometimes seem as high as the mortgage on your house. And, like the house, you can't get along without insurance.

Being part of a group is one way to cut the expense. Many local chambers of commerce offer health insurance at group rates, and so do many professional organizations. You might also try networking among other small business owners. Not all insurers charge the same rates, and because they share your problem small business owners may have already done the research to find the ones that cost the least.

You can also cut the cost of your medical insurance by going for a high-deductible policy. The premiums are lower, but remember you will be paying more money to a doctor or a hospital when you use it.

When you announce that you are open for business, you can count on getting letters and phone calls from all sorts of people trying to sell you something, and health insurance is high on the list, but be careful not to buy anything from anyone unless you are sure you are dealing with a reputable company, no matter how attractive the rate might seem. Remember the old rule that if something seems too good to be true, it probably is.

You might also want to consider investing in a pension plan so you'll be able to retire some day. Whatever your insurance needs, the good news is that it is all available from a single source, a good insurance agent. Like travel agents, these people don't charge fees either for advice or for looking out for your changing needs. Their income is from commissions on the premiums you pay year in and year out, so your insurance agent can be expected to be at your service as long as you are in business.

Be careful how you choose one. Look for an insurance agent who represents more than one company. Many do, and that gives you the advantage of being able to compare costs and coverages without going to several different sources. You'll also want an agent who is familiar with small businesses and can anticipate your needs. Chances are that the person who sold you your life insurance or homeowner's policies won't know what to make of this new life of yours. It's a good idea to talk with several different agents before you have one draw up your policies.

Remember that you are turning pro and you're going to need seasoned professionals behind you. Your lawyer, your accountant, and your insurance agent are going to be part of your team, so be careful to choose the right ones.

CHAPTER SEVEN

Finding Work

Most consultants agree that networking is the key to finding work, and many say that they've created websites to deliver information about themselves to prospects. But before they market their services, they must set fees, and this seems to be the number-one concern of every independent consultancy.

Barbara Arnold, an urban planner based in Buffalo, New York, says that when she works as a subcontractor for firms working for government agencies, the fee is generally established in advance and the assignment is made on a take-it-or-leave-it basis. Working directly for those government agencies on the other hand usually requires submitting a bid that will be competing with others for the lowest price. "Sometimes it's like a silent auction," Barbara says. "I don't know who is is bidding for the job, and I don't know how low their bid will be. But after you've been in this business for awhile, you get to know the competition and you get a feel for how they file bids." Very often historic preservation groups ask Barbara to tell them what she expects to be paid. "It's hard to do," she says. "I know what I need to earn to keep my business going, but I also know that these organizations operate on shoestring budgets. I never know what has been set aside for a project. Yes, of course, I can ask. But that seems unprofessional, at least to me. So it comes down to guesswork. Luckily, I seem to guess right most of the time. Still, I often wonder if I should have aimed higher."

It's one of those things you'll never know for sure, but sometimes it doesn't hurt to negotiate. Sandy Jones, who conducts seminars on parenting, finds that organizations that sponsor them seem to expect to do a little horse trading when it comes to integrating her fee into an overall program. Sandy also writes books and articles on parenting, and she learned early in the game never to accept a publisher's first offer, either. She took a course on negotiating she saw advertised in an in-flight magazine and she reports that it paid for itself with the first contract. She makes it a hard-and-fast rule to always ask for a third more than she thinks a client is prepared to pay, and to be prepared to back down slowly. In her experience, she has never had to back down by any amount even close to a third. "A third of what we do, whether it's selling a book idea or a chance to dispense advice for a fee, involves selling ourselves," she says. "You have to be able to take rejection in stride. We're a lot like T-shirt salesmen. Sometimes a hundred customers will look over what we have to sell before one buys. Then nine times out of ten, the one who does buy what we're selling doesn't even look at the price tag."

Determining the price tag for your consulting services may be the trickiest problem you're going to face when you start up on your own. Before you go out looking for clients, you need to know what you're going to charge, but figuring out how much that should be involves a thicket of variables—a nightmare—even for people who have been supporting themselves as consultants for decades.

When you are charging for consultancy services, there are no simple guidelines like the retail prices manufacturers suggest for the things they make. Especially when you are trying to get established, your fees need to be reasonable. But what does that mean? You can't charge too much or you won't get any business; charge too little and you'll soon be out of business.

When in doubt, remember the words of Lord Duveen, the art dealer who turned America's nineteenth-century robber barons into serious art collectors. Whenever any of them balked at his prices, he simply reminded them that "When you pay high for the priceless, you're getting it cheap."

WHAT'S THE GOING RATE?

Even if your specialty is something esoteric, such as advising people making offshore investments or guiding them through the political shoals of exporting goods from China or appraising illuminated manuscripts, you are not operating in a vacuum. Count on it, some people out there are specializing in something similar and they are good contacts in your search to determine the going rate. It can be a touchy business, though, because some people are uncomfortable discussing their earnings even with close friends. Others may be less than candid when you ask them how much they earn, and the answer to the old question "Does she or doesn't she?" may well be "Only her accountant knows for sure."

A good way to open dialogues with other consultants is through the Internet. The people you meet this way may be thousands of miles away but may be more forthcoming in sharing information with you. And don't forget to add their names to your Rolodex and encourage them to do the same with yours. As a consultant, your basic business will be sharing information and that means sharing with others in your own personal network.

You'll find that most consultants are open and helpful. It's the nature of their business, after all. They don't regard newcomers into their field as competition. Just be careful to ask about their fees and not about who their clients are. They may volunteer the information anyway, because as professionals the idea that someone would even think of stealing their business by cutting rates is as alien to them as the probability of a doctor trolling another doctor's waiting room for patients.

When you survey other consultants, though, keep in mind that style, skill, experience, and the nature of their practices are all factors that determine their rates. These are the same factors you will be considering, too. And as much depends on where you sell your work—what the traffic will bear—as the time and the effort that goes into it.

LET THE CLIENT BE YOUR GUIDE

The last item in your pricing survey is your potential clients, but this may be the trickiest one to handle. Ask anyone what they expect to pay for the help you're prepared to offer them and the answer is sure to be "As little as possible." On the other hand, at least among corporate clients, nothing happens until a budget has been established, and if you get close enough to a prospect, it may be possible to find out how much has been budgeted for the project you want to be involved with. Even armed with such insider information, don't forget to negotiate before you sign a contract. Most budgets have air built into them.

WHAT DO YOU NEED TO EARN?

Like your clients, you should run your business on a budget, too, and you need to do a bit of pencil-pushing before you agree to any price for a consulting assignment. Thanks to that business plan you put together, you have a clear idea of what it is costing you to deliver the goods. You know what it takes to keep your business running, from the electric bill to the phone bill to the grocery bill. Add it all up and you'll have a good idea what you need to earn in a month to keep body and soul together.

You can plan on working a lot of overtime and giving up your weekends, but for all practical purposes you have just twenty working days in a month. At eight hours a day, that adds up to one hundred sixty hours. However, you're going to need to spend a lot of that time marketing your services and traveling, among other things. You'll be invited to meetings, sometimes unexpectedly, where you'll be the only person in the room who isn't collecting a paycheck for being there. Although consultants with meeting-prone clients usually build the time involved into their fee, it is an unpredictable factor. But even in that best of all possible situations, you probably won't be able to count on more than one hundred twenty actual billable hours in any given month. Divide your costs by one hundred twenty and you'll have a rough idea of what you need to charge for an hour of your time just to break even. Most service businesses mark up that basic figure, which they call "direct labor," by 50 percent. So should you, to be sure you're making a profit.

Sometimes you may have to settle for less, to be sure, especially when you are establishing yourself, but make that basic hourly rate your goal at the beginning and it will take a lot of the guesswork out of the pricing dilemma.

CONSIDER THE VARIABLES

While you're pushing that pencil, go a step further to factor in some of the variables most consultants deal with. You'll have assignments that take longer than you anticipated and solutions that don't work out and need to be reworked. You may find problems neither you nor your client anticipated. Many consultants prepare for that in their original contracts by including contingency fees, but, in general, even minor second thoughts will take time to incorporate into your ultimate solution and from now on you need to remember that your time is your money.

Some clients may also take their own sweet time before sending you a check. It is standard among most consultants to ask for an advance retainer of up to half their total fee. They regard it is a test of a client's willingness to see the project to the finish, but most also point out that it takes all the financial worries out of the relationship. Some who collect advances go on to bill their clients by the hour as the project progresses. All of this, of course, must be spelled out in the original contract.

Although most consultants say they are usually paid for their work within a month, many large companies won't get your check into the mail for forty-five or more days. Remember, too, that their accounting departments won't even begin thinking about you until a bill has been submitted and gone through what can be a lengthy approval process. When you're living a day-to-day existence, as often happens when you're starting a new business, something like that can be worse than frustrating.

Don't forget as well that there will be seasonal cycles in your business and there are going to be months where you won't have enough work to keep you busy for one hundred twenty hours. Of course, you'll also have months when there won't be enough hours to get it all done. However, don't count on the times when you have to burn the midnight oil to even things out. If you were working for someone other than yourself, you'd expect to be paid for overtime, wouldn't you?

HOW WILL YOU CHARGE?

The hourly rate you establish for yourself will be the basis for setting fees for most of your assignments, though in many cases, consultants, and their clients too, prefer to come up with a bottom-line figure that reflects the amount of time they think it will take them to finish the job.

Jerry Held, who runs a small boutique advertising agency in Southern California, and whose business is advising small companies that have little experience with advertising and marketing, has seen his basic hourly rate double from thirty to sixty dollars since he started out in the early 1980s. His retail rate, for one-time clients, is twice as high. "I always charge by the project," he says, "because that is the only way a client knows up front what my services are going to cost. But if they request revisions with my creative output, I bill them by the hour."

Jerry cautions, "Before you quote any price, there are a few questions you need to ask yourself: Are your clients small businesses or big corporations? Is this assignment a one-time job or will there be repeat business that can make you comfortable with a lower hourly rate? After taking these things into account, I recommend that you shouldn't be either the cheapest or the most expensive option. Instead, make yourself the best value for a client's investment."

Again, some of your clients will enjoy having meetings. Often those meetings aren't really productive because they turn out to be little more than office get-togethers where the participants spend a lot of time sharing company gossip before they get to the point. While it may be an important way to get to know the people you are dealing with, you need to be sure that your fee reflects the time you'll be spending in that conference room. You won't always know before you submit a bid for an assignment whether the client is going to go overboard in scheduling meetings. When in doubt it is a good idea to either bump up your rate, or add hours to your estimate of how long you think the job will take. It can be frustrating to sit in endless unexpected meetings knowing that it is having a negative effect on your bottom line; not only that, but it can lead you to cut corners on the job itself, something you should never do.

No matter whether you charge by the hour or by the assignment, the fee you establish should be not so much for the job itself as for the results it will produce. As a consultant, you are in the business of results, and you should make that your top priority when you sit down with a client. Remember the old salesman's rule, "Sell the sizzle, not the steak."

ALWAYS HAVE A CONTRACT

It should go without saying that every assignment you take on should start with a contract that spells out both the things you are promising to do and the things your client expects of you. It doesn't have to be complicated, nor filled with arcane legal language. The simpler and more understandable it is, the better—that's especially true if your consultancy involves dealing with individuals rather than companies. If you are, say, planning to become a personal fitness trainer, a website designer, or a freelance editor, the people you will be dealing with may find contracts off-putting, but that doesn't mean you shouldn't insist on one. Just be careful to make it simple. And there is no law against making it friendly as long you touch all the bases.

Any price you quote in a contract is etched in stone. If it takes longer than you thought it would to complete an assignment, you can't go back and bump up the price. It is a good idea to build a contingency fee into your contract to cover yourself, but sometimes the extra time may involve changes the client makes along the way, which is another good reason to have a contract before you start—even a simple letter agreement is better than nothing. The point is to get it in writing.

Basically, your contract needs to spell out what you are expected to do, when the work is to begin and when it will end, and how and when you will be paid. It should also include whether your expenses are built into your fee or whether the client is expected to reimburse you. Your client, who needs to countersign the contract, may want to negotiate some of the points you make, but by the time you start the job, each of you will know exactly what to expect from the other.

THE COMPANY YOU KEEP

You've probably already given some thought to where you're going to find business—maybe it's a former employer who has indicated they can use your help.

Jim McClure started his consulting business working for the corporation that had just given him a buyout. Jim was lucky, however. In general, because of the tax laws, companies can't downsize by offering buyout packages and then go right on using the ex-employee as an independent contractor.

In Jim's case, the arrangement worked because his former employer was just one of a big portfolio of clients and the work he does for them now is with different subsidiary companies than the one he worked for as an employee. Jim didn't spread himself around to satisfy just an IRS rule, but he followed a rule that applies to every consultant in America—regardless of specialty: Having just one or two clients, no matter how big or how promising they may be, is like building a house on sand.

As accountant Irwin Fenichel puts it, "Concentration of risk, a small customer base, is something banks take a very dim view of and any small business owner needs to avoid it like the plague." No matter what your view of banks may be, that policy is right on the money. If you expect this new business of yours to support you for the rest of your life, never—ever—put all your eggs in one basket.

Starting out with a star client is the answer to everybody's dream, but it's like trying to start a fire with just one log in the fireplace. You need a couple more to produce anything more than sparks. You should ease into your business slowly, which means one client at a time; but no matter how tempting those big, almost full-time accounts may seem, don't make the mistake of trying to make it without building a family of clients.

Keep the family small at the beginning, but never stop planning for growth so that you can move forward as soon as you feel able to handle it.

WALK, DON'T RUN

One of the keys to success in starting any new business is to build it a buck at a time, but if you're like most people considering becoming an independent consultant, you've probably been solving other people's problems for quite a while. You know your field inside out, you know the people in it, and you might even have possible clients lined up waiting for you to declare your independence. You're raring to go.

These attributes—a thorough knowledge of your field, a network of other experts and contacts you've built developing your expertise—are the backbone of any consultancy. Despite all that, you should still move at a measured pace. At the very least, it will give you time to get used to life on your own and to explore related avenues of opportunity. You never know, this move you're making might mean more than just a change in your lifestyle, it could lead to a change in your focus. Suppose, for instance, that in your working life you mastered the intricacies of local building codes and then decided to turn that knowledge into an independent consultancy. A smart move, to be sure. But you may find along the way that some of your clients are looking for advice on construction management, a related field you may not have considered.

FINDING BUSINESS

Talk to an independent consultant about where business leads come from, and the answer most often will be "word of mouth." All through the life of your business, satisfied clients are going to be your very best source of new accounts.

But when you're starting out, you're going to need more than referrals. You'll need to get the word out to people who need your services but don't know you or anyone else you've worked with. To do that, you should develop a marketing plan that will help lead you to your prospects and turn them into clients.

Marketing plans are second nature to most big companies, and most consider them matters of life and death. You should, too, because it is your own future you are planning. You may have dealt with marketing plans in your former life, but it is possible that you are one of the millions who believe that "marketing" is just one of those words advertising agencies use in place of a perfectly good old-fashioned one, "selling." Yes, of course, it is selling, but there is more to it than that. Back in the 1960s, Neil Borden of the Harvard Business School invented the term "marketing mix" to describe the things that need to be blended together to make a marketing plan work. He summed up his definition in four words: Product, Place, Price, and Promotion. Product is the service you are offering and its benefit to a client. Place simply means location, and how it relates to your client's convenience. Price is not only what you charge, but how it translates to value for the client. Promotion includes all the things you do to get a prospect's attention, from advertising and public relations to the presentation that clinches the sale.

As you're developing your own marketing plan, you may find a few more words to describe your own special marketing mix. Among those might be "packaging," something very important if you were marketing a new brand of canned soup, but which applies to your service business, too, in terms of the name you give your practice, the logo you have designed, and the appearance of your business cards and stationery. Another related term is the "personality" of your business. It is a reflection of your own personality, of course, but it also involves your professional image and the way clients view your practice. Such things are all part of the marketing mix, and they all need careful planning before you open for business.

CHECK OUT THE NUMBERS

The way professional marketers begin to find their targets is by studying statistics, beginning with those they call demographics. It is simply a study of where people live, how they make their living, and what their lifestyle is like. The numbers, and names, that apply to your personal universe are usually available at the local library or through the chamber of commerce or some similar business organization. Your demographic research will give you some insight into the potential market for your services.

Those numbers are especially important to consultancies that offer personal services to individuals, such as fitness training or financial advice; they will give you breakdowns by age and sex as well as income. If you are contemplating advising retirees on investments, you'll want to be sure that senior citizens haven't taken their money elsewhere to another part of the country.

Another set of statistics marketers treasure is what large marketing strategists call "psychographics," the information that gives them clues about what makes people buy one product or service over another. Using surveys and focus groups, large organizations get information that helps them come up with what the advertising community calls a "unique selling proposition," the plan that helps set their products apart from the competition and turn prospects into loyal customers.

Unless you are one yourself, small business people like you don't have the resources to hire marketing consultants to help them arrive at such conclusions, but you might not even need one. Because your business will be small at the beginning, you'll be in closer contact with the people you are serving. Every meeting with a client should be a mini-focus group. Keep your ears open and you'll probably learn something more than just the details of the assignment at hand. Listen to enough of them, and you'll know what you are doing right. Then lead with those strengths in the proposals, the mailing pieces, and everything else that comes out of your marketing plan aimed at building new business.

BUILDING A BRAND

Identifying potential clients is only half the battle when you're putting together a marketing plan. The other half, targeting and reaching them, may be even more important.

As a consultant, your approach to every client's situation is as unique to you as the shape of your nose. But don't expect prospects to notice that on their own. Make their decision easy: Build an image for yourself. Calling attention to your style and to your approach, whether you're an economist or an antiques appraiser, can make all the difference in a client's decision whether to hire you or someone else with similar ideas. Yes, you need to start with an idea, but ideas are only as good as what you propose to do with them.

Keep in mind that what you're actually selling is what your expertise can do for people. The bottom line or personal style may be important when someone decides to hire one consultant over another, but in the end it's what they're getting for their money that is most important.

IT MAY PAY TO ADVERTISE

When you're putting your marketing plan together, the advertising sales people at local newspapers and magazines, radio and television stations are prime sources of information about the local business community. All have media kits filled with information about the people they reach. Much of it can be priceless in your search for the people you ought to be reaching, too.

Most consultants advertise their services, even if on a limited, targeted basis. Vickie Sherman says that she runs ads in local newspapers and occasionally in business magazines, but she says she does it "not necessarily to generate business but to establish credibility and name recognition." The name she chose for her human resources consultancy, Human Dynamics, is one that not only says what she does but isn't easily forgotten.

Like many other consultants, Vickie also lists her company on some of the several job-search sites on the Internet. Michael Nelson has found new clients that way, and he has also put up his own web site to keep the business coming in. You can find the job-search sites and a lot of related web pages under the key word "consultants" when you sign on. There is usually no charge to add your own listing and, although it isn't a sure thing, there are opportunities there.

SELLING BY MAIL

Not every sales call you make is going to get business for you—at least not right now—but that doesn't mean it won't pay off somewhere down the road. It's a matter of keeping in touch.

Jim McClure, whose consultancy specializes in crisis management, routinely sends letters to executives whose promotions have been announced in the business press. "It's a simple letter," he says, "that invites them to 'think of me if you get in a crunch,' and it works."

Beth D'Addono, a public relations consultant, is pleased to report that, "A current job I have, one or two days a week at a $250 day rate, came from a direct mailing I sent out. I mailed 20 letters to people I hadn't heard from in a while and got eight responses. One of them turned into this job."

As anyone in the direct-mail business will tell you that is an almost unheard-of response rate. Beth adds that in addition to the fact that it was "a great letter," it also went to people who knew her but needed to be reminded of her availability and her interest. If you don't believe the axiom "out of sight, out of mind" yet, you're going to come to understand exactly what it means when you become an independent consultant.

Among the prospects who respond to your reminders that you are still alive and kicking, some are going to say, "Thanks, but no thanks," but that doesn't mean you've lost them forever. Save their names in your computer and keep in touch with them. Maybe you'll you'll find a business solution down the road that would interest them. When you do, drop them a note telling them you thought they'd be interested. They very well might be.

FREE ADVERTISING

One of these days you're going to bump into a prospect on the street or in the checkout line at the supermarket—it may be someone you've worked with before or a friend who once promised to use your service but so far has neglected to. "I've been meaning to call you," the person will gush. Then you'll exchange business cards and when you follow up you'll have an assignment you hadn't expected.

That person might have called you long ago if you had sent a letter to all your friends, acquaintances, and former associates telling them about your new business. Such a letter doesn't have to be an out-and-out solicitation, but rather a "wish me luck" kind of thing. Just don't forget to include a subtle suggestion that you are offering a service they might be able to use someday. You should make it a point to send letters to all of your former associates because those contacts are going to be your stock-in-trade as a consultant, and they are key to your reputation.

Suppose you hadn't been on that street corner at that precise moment or decided to put off the grocery shopping. Do you think they'd have called you? Probably not. But you can't be everywhere and you can't expect to bump into business every time you drop by the local coffeeshop. (However, don't *ever* leave home without a supply of business cards!)

An important thing to remember when you are looking for new business is that it is a rare thing for prospects to call you unless you do something to nudge them first.

PRESS RELEASES

There are a few ways you can keep your name out there even when you are hard at work taking care of your existing business. One of them is to send out press releases to local newspapers and to trade papers in your field. You should do it when you start up your new business, of course, but also every time you sign a new contract.

As a consultant, you are by definition an expert in a particular field. But not everybody knows that yet. Get to know reporters who write about your field and encourage them to put your name on their Rolodexes for your input and quotes on new developments. Once they get to know you—and it doesn't hurt to encourage that—they'll call you. And they'll use your name in stories they write. That, of course, builds your credibility faster than almost anything else you can do.

USE BROADCASTERS

Broadcast reporters and personalities also make it their business to come up with "experts" to add credibility to the things they are reporting, and you need to let them know that you are an accessible expert in your field. There is no magic involved. Their producers keep files of contacts in every field imaginable, from architecture to economics, and when they need an expert they simply pick up the phone. It all begins for you when you pick up the phone and call the broadcaster's office to find the producer who will interview you. Once you've done that, you may have to wait a while for your big break. That's show business. But you're going to find it's well worth it.

SELL YOURSELF

Everybody knows that a client who is pleased with your work is going to become a repeat customer. However, keeping the customer satisfied goes beyond delivering dynamite solutions to their problems. As the old song says, "It Ain't What You Do, It's the Way That You Do it."

The most important thing you can do is make your clients feel important. That may seem too obvious to mention, but the business world is a lot less personal today than it once was and old-fashioned courtesy seems to have become just that—an old-fashioned idea—but you can easily turn that into an advantage. In a world where there is so little of it, simple courtesy can stand out like a summer sunrise. It doesn't take any effort and it doesn't cost anything. Just a simple "thank you" for the business can work wonders.

A friendly attitude also can go a long way with everyone you deal with. When you visit a client's office, for instance, don't rush past the receptionist without stopping to chat for a minute or so. One of the first things you are going to learn as a consultant is that you have to be a good listener, and there are going to be times when you'll get more information from the outer office than from the inner sanctum. But that notwithstanding, it is gesture that will be probably be remembered when the time comes that you have to interrupt a client's meeting for an important call that can't wait.

The fact is, everybody in an office you visit is as important as the person you've gone there to see. For instance, some of those people are going to be promoted one of these days and others are likely to move to different companies. Make sure they'll remember you.

NETWORK YOUR WAY TO NEW BUSINESS

Establishing a network simply means keeping in touch with old friends and associates as often as you can. It also means making new contacts by meeting people face-to-face whenever possible. Nobody will go to a stranger when they already know someone who can give them help when they need it.

Even if some of the people you meet at parties or meetings may never need a consultant with a speciality such as yours, it is a good bet that if you make the right impression on them, they'll be your biggest booster among friends who might. People take great pleasure in recommending sources to friends. "Hey, I know someone who can easily solve that problem for you," is one of the friendliest statements there is because it connects friends who might otherwise remain strangers. And sometimes it is surprising where big long-range assignments come from.

DEVELOP CENTERS OF INFLUENCE

At some point in your life, maybe when you got married or promoted in your job, you probably had a call from a life insurance agent. When you finally agreed to listen to the sales pitch, you may have discovered that your best friend sicced him on you. Then, as you signed on the dotted line, the agent casually asked if you had any other friends who might need coverage. Of course you did, and the agent had some new leads. That technique, called "centers of influence," has sold billions of dollars' worth of life insurance over the years. It's another form of networking.

It can work wonders for you, too. If a client praises your work, don't be a shrinking violet. Ask for a success letter that you can forward to your prospects. And don't forget to ask for the name of someone else who should know what you can do for them. Either approach might get you your next assignment.

People in today's business world are likely to have worked for several different companies before landing at the desk where you caught up with them. They often know other people with needs and problems similar to theirs and they don't usually mind sharing sources with them. As you get to know your clients, you'll get a feel for who might be forthcoming and who might be put off by a request for a referral, but chances are you're going to find a lot more of the former than the latter.

BE A JOINER

Over most of the country's history, professional salespeople measured their success by the number of organizations they belonged to. They may not have called it networking, but they all regarded it as the best way to make customers out of strangers.

When Debra Jason established her direct marketing business in Colorado, she had just arrived from New York and was a relative stranger in town. She made it a point to join as many organizations as she had time for, from the local chamber of commerce to the Rocky Mountain Direct Marketing Association, of which she became president. But, she says, "Joining isn't enough. You have to get involved. I write articles for organization newsletters and recently after I gave a speech at a chamber of commerce meeting, one of the members asked me to repeat it for his sales staff and I earned a nice fee." And where do think that sales manager has turned for marketing consultation ever since?

Whether you become a joiner or not depends on the prospects you need to target, the kinds of organizations that are in your area, and your own personality. It makes good sense to join local business groups that are likely to have potential clients in their membership, and most consultants find it important to get involved with business and professional organizations that reflect their specialities. It generally pays off in priceless networking opportunities, but there is another advantage: meeting other people in your field will give you a chance to share ideas, as well as frustrations, with other people who are in the same boat as you.

You'll also meet a lot of people and make good contacts by joining sales and marketing groups and signing up for their seminars. In your new life, no matter what kind of consulting you are doing, you are going to be in the sales business, too, and there is no reason why you shouldn't be as professional at it as you are in your consultancy practice.

TRY VOLUNTEERING

Another thing you might consider is volunteering some of your time at such institutions as the local library. This will instantly connect you with others from your community and you might be surprised at *who else* is volunteering. Just give careful thought to the kinds of organizations you want to support. If you're looking for work as a landscape architect, for example, you might offer to redesign a tired garden in a visible public space or offer your skills to a community garden.

Be leery, though, about volunteering your consulting services. Your forays into pro bono work can easily get out of hand. Be careful that you don't find yourself spending more time than you intended handling things you'd otherwise get paid for.

WORKING FOR THE GOVERNMENT

Back in the days of the New Deal and on through World War II, the federal government hired hundreds of business leaders as consultants. They were called "dollar-a-year men" because of the fees they were paid. In the years since, the number of consultants working in the so-called public sector has grown to the hundreds of thousands and the fees they collect have grown dramatically, too.

Depending on your specialty, working for the government as a consultant makes very good sense. And the list of specialties that federal, state, and local governments are looking for will surprise you. There are some differences between doing business with them than with private companies, but the maze of rules the government follows is relatively easy to negotiate because it has established ways to guide you through it.

Many government contracts begin with an Invitation for Bids (IFB), which spells out what is needed. Forms are provided and submitted in sealed envelopes. When they are opened, the job goes to the low bidder, as long as that bidder is qualified to do the job. Others are begun with a Request for Proposals (RFP), which is more like a fishing expedition on the part of the government agency. Respondents are asked to describe how they'd approach the problem and the ultimate contract is awarded more for merit than price.

There are several ways to find out about these requests and invitations. In the case of federal agencies, the General Services Administration maintains Business Services Centers in most large cities. They will place your name on mailing lists, steer you to publications that will help you do business with the government, and show you how the system works.

The Small Business Administration (SBA) is another valuable source of information. The mission of its procurement centers is to make sure that small businesses win as many government contracts as possible. In many cases, they also steer small businesses to large prime contractors to obtain subcontracting opportunities. Among the ways it keeps track of qualified applicants is a program it calls the Procurement Automated Source System (PASS). Getting into the database is as simple as filling out a form, available at every SBA office, that will result in a profile of what your consultancy has to offer.

The Government Printing Office is at your service, too. Among the publications it offers is the *Commerce Business Daily*, published five times a week by the Department of Commerce to keep you up to the minute on opportunities for government contracts. Its catalog also includes a host of publications that explain not only the regulations involved but also who makes buying decisions and how to prepare your bids. Many of them are also available on CD-ROM.

KEEP UP WITH THE FUTURE

It should go without saying that the only way you can expect to have a future as an expert in your field is to stay on top of every development in that field. You can do it through trade journals, of course, and from networking with other consultants, too. But don't overlook clients who may be exploring changes themselves. "Talking shop" is the best way there is to keep up with trends. Just remember that it is a two-way conversation. Share your knowledge as freely as you can. And don't forget to keep your ears open.

No matter what your specialty may be, it is certain that it is evolving, and if you expect to be effective you are going to need to stay informed. That means lots of browsing in bookstores and on the Internet, not just to research the job at hand, but to keep your eye on the future.

Remember that when all is said and done, you are in the idea business and the only way to succeed is to keep your own ideas fresh and timely. It is what your competitors will be doing, and what your clients will expect of you.

They will also expect you to keep up with the changing tools of the trade and be equipped with the technology they consider basic but may not have seemed so important a few years back. In the 1970s a study conducted for corporate purchasing agents concluded that although fax machines were "useful in libraries

and newspaper offices, they do not have any practical applications in the business world." Of course, that was a long time ago,
but it demonstrates the danger of making assumptions. No one
knows what obscure business applications will change from today's frill to tomorrow's necessity. When you are running your
own business, you are going to need to keep your eyes open to
anticipate changes in the way business is done.

CHAPTER EIGHT

Do I Have a Business?

Once the start-up phase of your consultancy business and its day-to-day operation has become routine, step back and take a look at how your life has changed. Taking inventory is crucial to seeing what works, what doesn't, and how you might do things differently to improve your new life. Sometimes the most obvious things are difficult to see when you're racing to complete an assignment or struggling to find new ones.

AM I FINDING THE SATISFACTION I HOPED FOR?

Satisfaction is a goal—and it can be an elusive one at the start of any new business. There are few businesses of any kind out there that don't experience any hardship whatsoever, so consider it part of the package of your new venture.

It may be possible that you've become disenchanted because you are overwhelmed with work and don't see any end to it. It may be that the work that has become your niche has been taking more time than you anticipated. If that is the case, you might be able to get around the problem by shifting the focus of your new business to something that is less labor-intensive.

If long, unrewarding hours are standing between you and happiness, try to schedule small vacations every now and then. A long weekend away from your clients and your work without your laptop and cell phone can work wonders in restoring your energy and your enthusiasm. Yes, the meter stops when you go away, and not only will you not be earning any money for a couple of days, but you'll be spending it instead. However, it was a heavy workload that painted you into this corner, and R&R is the secret way out.

Sometimes the overload would've been avoidable if you hadn't put unpleasant tasks on the back burner and later found them boiling over. If procrastination is among your problems—and it's one of the most common ones—consider scheduling your more tiresome tasks early in the day to get them out of the way. It will give you a chance to look forward to the things you need to accomplish during the rest of the afternoon.

Many consultants find there is more demand for what they do than there are hours in the day. It is tempting to grab at every opportunity that comes your way, especially at the beginning, but you should make it a point not to take on more work than you can comfortably handle. To be sure, it isn't easy to say "no" to a job offer, but remember that you are in business for the long haul. It is very likely there are more offers where those came from, and they'll come at times when you can more comfortably fit them into your schedule.

Remember, too, that when you are dealing with more work than you can easily handle, the quality of your solutions to clients' problems will suffer because of the pressure. Your reputation is your number-one asset and you need to give your undivided attention to every assignment because it will show in the results if you don't.

You've come a long way with this business of yours, so if things don't seem to be working quite right, fight hard to come up with creative answers. Sometimes tiny changes can have a big impact on small businesses. One of the reasons why there are so many opportunities for consultants these days is that nobody has all the answers, so if you are really stumped, look for answers by networking among friends and associates. Jim O'Reilly, who runs an advertising business in the Baltimore area, points out that, "Like most others in this business, I have been helped by someone in my past. I can remember pathetic looks from creative directors who stooped to tell me how to put an idea portfolio together, 'Tear out that bad ad and do it right; tear out a good ad in a series and get on with the next one in the series. Demonstrate that you can do this job.' None of us would be where we are without someone's help, and most of us are willing to repay the favor."

Usually it doesn't take very long to find answers to your problems. All it takes is a look at them through someone else's eyes. You are in the business of advice, after all. Don't be too proud to ask for some once in a while. It can make all the difference.

AM I MAKING OR LOSING MONEY?

Knowing whether you're making or losing money as a consultant isn't always easy because the biggest commodity you're dealing with is your time. That doesn't lend itself to a balance sheet that compares money you've spent to money you've earned.

Except for those who deal with financial matters in their business, a surprising number of independent consultants don't have a clue how much money they're making until their accountant puts the numbers together at tax time. Sometimes it's a pleasant surprise, sometimes not. You're often too busy making money to take the time to keep track of it. And for some, making it to the end of the month with enough to pay the bills is all that seems to matter. But your living expenses and your company's overhead can get out of hand if you're not careful.

Just about every small business has cash-flow problems at one time or another, and your consultancy practice isn't going to be immune to it. After you've been in your own business for awhile, you may notice that bill collecting is a big part of it, even though you didn't consider it important to your original job description. Sometimes the question isn't whether you're making or losing money, but when are those checks going to arrive? Then there are times when your receivables don't match your expenses. At times like these you need to make a realistic appraisal of your future as a consultant and whether you can afford to be one.

However, you may not have collection problems at all in your new business. Most consultants say they don't. Many say they can count on being paid within a month of billing, except for big corporate clients that take longer. It is also common practice for consultants to build advance retainers into their contracts, and that does away with a lot of collection problems for them, but there is another side to that coin.

It requires a great deal of self-discipline to deposit a big advance into your bank account and not be tempted to spend it before the next check comes along. It's human nature to look at a big bank balance and begin spending like there's no tomorrow, but you have to remember that the purpose of the advance is to tide you over during the weeks and possibly months before you can begin collecting the balance of your fee. Always keep in mind that an advance is a cushion and not a gift and that you're going to need to earn that money before any more comes along. Probably the easiest solution is to divide the funds into weekly increments and pay yourself a salary at the end of each week. Just be careful not to borrow from next week's allotment when you do.

IS IT TIME TO MODIFY MY ORIGINAL PLAN?

If, after time, you find that your business plan isn't producing as much income, or as much satisfaction, as you had hoped, the solution may be to use your skills in a different way.

That doesn't necessarily mean that you should think about

starting over again from scratch. Your core business interests you or you wouldn't have considered it in the beginning, but there may be ways to bring other interests into the picture to enhance your life as an independent businessperson.

Karen Gravelle was working for a health care provider when the AIDS epidemic broke out, and because she found herself in at the ground floor as the search began for a cure, she began marketing her knowledge to pharmaceutical companies who needed to be kept informed of developments in the field. She has more assignments than she can handle and she loves doing them. But she keeps her mental batteries charged by backing away from it once in a while. "I have a short attention span," she reveals, "and I get my mind back on track writing children's books. I get just as much satisfaction from it as I do working with doctors and researchers, although not nearly as much money. I didn't plan for my sideline at the beginning, it just happened, but it has been a lifesaver."

IS THIS THE LIFE FOR ME?

No matter how promising your business may seem at the beginning, you may find after time that it's a better idea to cut your losses. It isn't a sign of failure, but rather a realistic approach to improving your life.

Michael Nelson is running a very successful consulting practice today, but when he first graduated from college he and his wife, who had gone to law school, established a consultancy specializing in legal research and it failed. "We made a big mistake in our choice of location," he recalls. "Our service was unique to Des Moines, where we established the business, but the legal community there wasn't big enough to support us. We decided early in the game to admit we had made a mistake, and began looking for full-time jobs. The way it turned out, I found one that taught me the intricacies of human resources, a field that

interested me. Other jobs that followed gave me even more experience and I'm using that today in my consultancy. But if we
hadn't admitted defeat back in Des Moines, Kathy and I would
probably still be dealing with a single specialty."

DO I SEE A BRIGHT FUTURE?

If you aren't finding the income or the satisfaction you were
expecting, analyze the possibilities of making the future brighter.
It took a lot of faith and courage to start up your own business
in the first place and the same qualities that kept you going then
can help you turn it in the right direction now.

No business enterprise is a sure thing, but in terms of con-
trolling their own destinies, thousands have discovered that being
an independent consultant is as good as it gets. There are pot-
holes along the way, but with foresight most of the deep ones
can be avoided.

If a major client suddenly goes out of business, hopefully
you've been cultivating options along the way. If you forsee competition mushrooming all around you, be ready to alter your plan
and develop a new specialty. One of the beauties of a consulting
business is that there are so many potential niches within each
specialty.

The future never takes care of itself in anybody's life, but when
all is said and done, if you keep your eye on it and plan for
it, your future as a consultant can be brighter than you ever
imagined.

Get ready to have fun making a living for a change. If you are
like most people who have found a second life as a consultant,
you are going to find yourself looking back someday and asking,
"Why didn't I do this sooner?"